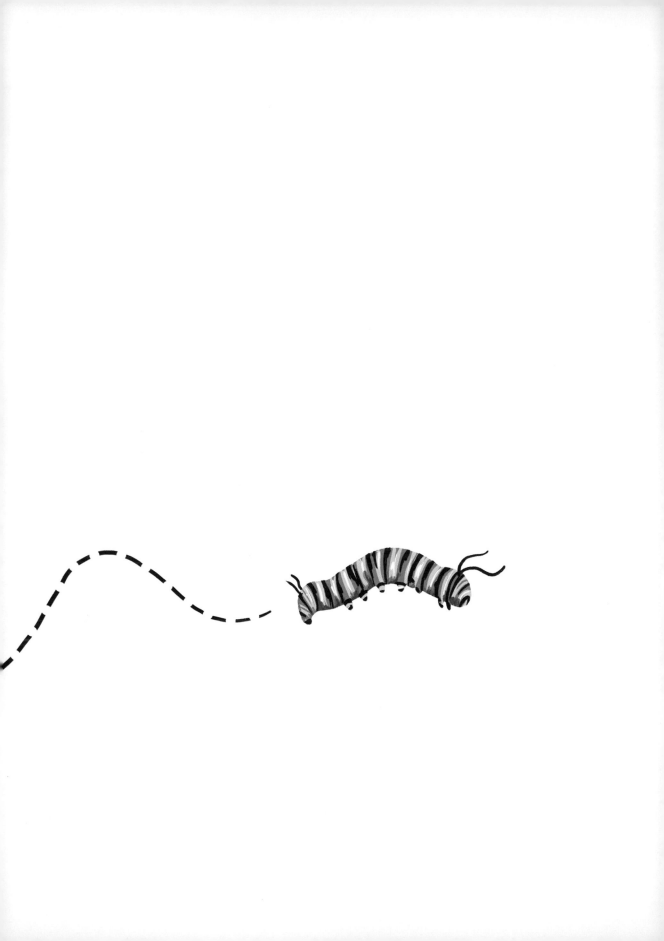

YOU CAN
LIVE
ON THE
BRIGHT SIDE

THE KIDS' GUIDE TO OPTIMISM

LUCY BELL

Also by Lucy Bell

You Can Change the World:

The Kids' Guide to a Better Planet

YOU CAN
LIVE
ON THE
BRIGHT
SIDE

THE
KIDS' GUIDE
TO OPTIMISM

LUCY BELL

Andrews McMeel
PUBLISHING®

Andrews McMeel Publishing
a division of Andrews McMeel Universal
1130 Walnut Street, Kansas City, Missouri 64106

www.andrewsmcmeel.com

First published in Australia in 2021 by Pantera Press Pty Limited
P.O. Box 1989, Neutral Bay, NSW, Australia 2089

22 23 24 25 26 SHO 10 9 8 7 6 5 4 3 2 1

ISBN: 978-1-5248-7552-7

Library of Congress Control Number: 2021952350

Cover Design and Illustrations: Astred Hicks
Editor: Melissa R. Zahorsky
Art Director: Julie Barnes
Production Editor: Brianna Westervelt
Production Manager: Carol Coe

Made by:
Shanghai Offset Printing Products LTD.
Plant 1, No. 39 HengLing North Road, NianFeng Community,
PingDi Subdistrict, LongGang District, Shenzhen,
Guangdong Province, China 518110
First printing
June 2022

FSC
www.fsc.org
MIX
Paper from
responsible sources
FSC® C109093

ATTENTION: SCHOOLS AND BUSINESSES

Andrews McMeel books are available at quantity discounts with
bulk purchase for educational, business, or sales promotional use.
For information, please e-mail the Andrews McMeel Publishing
Special Sales Department: specialsales@amuniversal.com.

To James,
my sunshine through the clouds,
who always laughs the loudest.

This day was only the first of many similar ones for the emancipated Mole, each of them longer and fuller of interest as the ripening summer moved onward. He learned to swim and to row, and entered into the joy of running water; and with his ear to the reed stems he caught, at intervals, something of what the wind went whispering so constantly among them.

KENNETH GRAHAME
THE WIND IN THE WILLOWS

CONTENTS

DO YOU EVER WAKE UP in the morning, look out your window to see the sun shining, and you can't wait to get started on the day? Maybe there's something you're excited about doing, whether it's seeing friends, going for a bike ride, or reading your favorite book. Maybe it's as simple as eating something yummy for breakfast! Whatever it is, you just know that today is going to be a good day.

This is called optimism, or positivity, and it's such a nice feeling to have. It's also something that you can learn, practice, and improve, so you can feel that way more often.

Optimism is about feeling hopeful, lighter, and looking forward to your day, week, or even something that's months away. It's about looking on the bright side of life, so you can live on the bright side.

The world is big, busy, and bustling. There's so much to keep on top of every day, it can sometimes feel overwhelming. How many times a day does someone tell you to hurry up? Everyone always seems to be in a rush!

The following pages are filled with tips, tricks, tools, activities, and recipes. They'll help you slow down and find time for the things that make you excited to leap out of bed each morning, ready to do more of what you love, and find out what makes you uniquely you.

Life is full of ups and downs. No one can be optimistic all the time, so it's all right to feel a bit low sometimes. We all have days where we feel tired and just want to curl up in bed with a good book and a mug of hot chocolate.

It can be easy to look around and think that everyone else is having an easier time. But feeling blue is normal for everyone. We all face different struggles and often people will hide their emotions, so it can be difficult to tell when others are feeling down. There will always be times when things don't feel like they're going our way, or we feel a bit gloomy and can't explain why. Sometimes, this is because we haven't slept well, we haven't been eating enough healthy food, we haven't been spending enough time outdoors, or because there are lots of things we need to get done and we feel anxious.

When you're doing something unfamiliar or that makes you uncomfortable, like starting at a new school, trying a new sport, or speaking in front of lots of people, it's okay to feel worried about it. We all have self-doubt, and can lose confidence in ourselves—even the bravest warriors feel afraid sometimes.

If you lose something or someone you love, you will feel sad for a while, and that's okay. These times can be tough, but it's important to know that they don't last forever. The world will become brighter again. The sun will poke through the clouds.

It's important to know that if you're feeling blue too often, and can't stop worrying about things, then there are people you can turn to for support. Talking about things with the right person can get the worries out of your head, and some people are trained to help you do this. So don't be afraid to speak to someone you trust and ask for help.

Remember too that knowing what it's like to feel sad or anxious means we can understand better when other people are having a tough time. We might even be able to comfort them. We're all in this together.

Even on the gloomy days, there's always room for us to learn more about what makes us happy. This book is full of ideas for living in a way where you feel the happiest and healthiest you can be. And who knows, by using some of these ideas, or coming up with some of your own, you might even turn a bad day into a good one!

You don't have to do all the things in this book to live on the bright side. It's designed to show you how to find the things you enjoy. If you try writing a poem and think it's totally boring, but you love cooking, throw your poem out the window and get into the kitchen. Or maybe today's the day to go for a run, not sit inside and meditate. You get to choose what you want to do!

There are so many things to love about the world—we just have to take the time to notice them.

ACTIVITY

In the morning, write down three things you're looking forward to today.

Then at night, write down the three things you enjoyed doing most today. Are they the same as the three things you wrote down in the morning, or did you find something new you enjoyed doing?

MIND

DID YOU KNOW?

The average person spends 92 days
on the toilet in their lifetime. That's
a lot of time to sit and think!

ONE OF THE FIRST STEPS to living on the bright side is learning to calm your mind. Our brains are busy bees. Even when we're not aware of it, they're constantly working on processing new information, solving problems, deciding what we want for lunch, planning what we're going to do tomorrow, worrying about stuff, reminding us to do things, and making sure our bodies are working properly. All these thoughts and processes can send our brains into a big tizzy! This can make it very difficult to concentrate on one thing at a time. Sometimes you might wish you had an "off" switch to shut down your brain for a while!

The exercises and activities here will show you how to slow down. This will help you become more relaxed and aware of your surroundings. It's nice to take your time and enjoy the little things in life—like eating an orange, listening to the birds, or checking to see what color the sky is today.

MINDFULNESS

MINDFULNESS IS ABOUT SLOWING DOWN, not rushing from one thing to the next, and really noticing what you're doing right now. It's about observing what you're thinking, feeling, and doing in this moment, not going over what you did yesterday or wondering what's going to happen tomorrow. The aim of mindfulness is to learn to focus on the present, and experience each moment as it happens throughout the day. For many people, this can lead to more feelings of happiness, joy, and positivity.

Sometimes mindfulness happens all on its own, like when you're playing a game and not thinking about anything else. Maybe you're playing tennis and all you're thinking about is taking your next shot. Or you might be reading a book and you become so immersed in the world inside its pages that you forget about the outside world.

Mindfulness is a way of living, and the more you practice it, the better at it you get!

Being mindful is a wonderful feeling because you're fully focused yet it takes no effort at all. It feels easy and you find yourself enjoying things more than usual. It can also help you become calm again when you're angry, upset, or worried.

Try some of the mindfulness activities here and find out which is your favorite way to feel peaceful and focused. If it doesn't work right away, that's okay; we can't be peaceful all the time—sometimes you probably want to be noisy!

MINDFUL EATING

Get a snack or a serving of your favorite food, then find somewhere comfortable to sit. Make sure your shoulders, arms, and legs are relaxed. Now, look at your food. What color and shape is it? How big is it? Is it a full meal or just a snack? Imagine yourself eating it and notice if your tummy reacts. Is it sending hunger signals? Is it growling as though a tiger is living in there? Now, give your food a good sniff. Does the smell remind you of anything? Does it make you picture a time or place? For example, the smell of a juicy sun-ripened orange when you first start to peel it might remind you of sitting in the sunshine on a summer afternoon. When you put the food in your mouth, what feeling do you notice? Do you have a tingling in your mouth like you want to start biting into the food? What about its temperature: is it hot or cold or room temperature? Is the texture soft, chewy, or crunchy? As you chew, does the taste and texture change? Now your tummy probably feels ready to receive some delicious food!

MINDFUL LISTENING

Play your favorite song and try to experience it in a new way. See if you can pick out the instruments, learn the words, or tap along with the drum beat. Search the internet for other things to listen to for mindfulness. Some good sounds are wind chimes, bells, or singing bowls. Maybe you even have your own bells or chimes at home! Focus on the sound of a bell as it rings out and resonates. Listen carefully as it slowly fades away until you can no longer hear it.

You can also listen to sounds around you, such as rain falling on the roof, wind whispering through the trees, a train rumbling by, people out and about on the street, the traffic, a baby crying nearby, or a neighbor practicing their violin. Observe all the sounds as they come and go.

GO ON A WONDER WALK ———————————————————

Next time you're out for a walk, look around at all the things you've never noticed before that you can wonder about. If you're in the bush, look at the kind of path you're walking on—is the soil damp, or dry and stony? Maybe there are tree roots winding across the trail, or perhaps there are stairs built into the rocks. Can you see any plants, wildlife, or insects that you've never noticed before? Sometimes there are mushrooms dotted along the path, or squirrels hiding in the brush. What can you hear? You might hear birds singing, flies buzzing, trees rustling, and the crunching of leaves beneath your feet. And what can you smell? Depending where you are, you might catch the damp earthiness of a forest floor, the dry dustiness of the desert, or the honey-sweet smell of native flowers.

If you go on a walk around your neighborhood, you might notice fancy mailboxes you don't remember seeing before, decorative lampposts, beautifully tended garden beds, fallen leaves, or chalk drawings that kids have left behind. Maybe you'll hear a lawnmower, an airplane overhead, or someone vacuuming their house; and maybe you'll smell a curry cooking, muffins baking, freshly mown grass, the pavement as it heats up in the sun, or—in winter—woodfire smoke coming from chimneys.

There are so many things going on around us if we only take a moment to notice them.

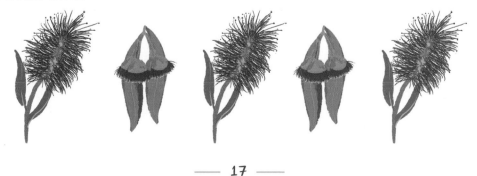

TIP

When you're feeling upset, try to name your feelings one by one using the simplest words you can think of, such as "confused," "sad," "angry," "disappointed," and so on. As we grow up, we get better at identifying our emotions. This is called emotional awareness. It helps us understand ourselves better, and know what we want and don't want.

STOP

IF YOU FIND YOURSELF FEELING A LITTLE OVERWHELMED, ANXIOUS, OR WORRIED, IT CAN SOMETIMES BE HELPFUL TO STOP:

S = STOP WHAT YOU'RE DOING FOR A MOMENT. YOU CAN CLOSE YOUR EYES IF YOU WANT TO.

T = TAKE A FEW DEEP BREATHS. FOCUS ON THE BREATH COMING IN AND OUT OF YOUR NOSE.

O = OBSERVE WHAT'S HAPPENING INSIDE AND OUTSIDE OF YOU. WHAT ARE YOU THINKING AND FEELING? SEE IF YOU CAN NAME YOUR EMOTIONS. REMEMBER THAT THOUGHTS ARE NOT FACTS.

P = PROCEED WITH SOMETHING THAT WILL MAKE YOU FEEL BETTER. THIS MIGHT BE CONTINUING WITH WHAT YOU WERE DOING IF YOU FEEL OKAY TO DO SO, OR IT MIGHT BE TALKING TO A FRIEND OR YOUR PARENTS, GOING FOR A WALK, OR LISTENING TO MUSIC.

ACTIVITY: MAKE A MIND JAR

A mind jar works like a snow globe: when you shake it up, there's a storm inside. Then, if you watch as the storm slowly calms down, you might find you calm down too. If you're feeling angry or upset, give the jar a shake and watch as everything that's been swirled up then begins to fall into place. Remind yourself that even when things go wrong, everything will settle back down and be okay. There are many ups and downs in life.

Here's how to make your own mind jar

What you'll need:

- ❀ a repurposed jar
- ❀ warm water
- ❀ liquid glycerin
- ❀ 1 teaspoon dishwashing liquid
- ❀ 2 tablespoons glitter (ideally biodegradable)
- ❀ food coloring in your favorite color

What to do:

1. Fill your jar 2/3 of the way with warm water.
2. Add the glycerin until the jar is almost full, then add the dishwashing liquid.
3. Stir in the glitter and about 3 drops of food coloring (you hardly need any).
4. Screw the lid of the jar on tight and get shaking!

TIP

If you start to feel overwhelmed, pay attention to your thoughts. Make sure they're positive ones and not unhelpful ones. For example, if you have a big school assignment to do, and you start to feel panicked, you might think *This is impossible* or *I'll never be able to do this.* These are unhelpful thoughts. When you notice them happening, try to change them to helpful ones, such as *Maybe it would help if I break it down into smaller sections* or *Maybe there's someone I can ask for help* or *If I take a break, maybe I'll feel better.*

MEDITATION IS ONE WAY YOU can experience mindfulness. While mindfulness is a way of living and it happens throughout the day, meditation is an activity where you set aside time to practice techniques to train your awareness. Through meditation, you can develop many different qualities, including mindfulness, better sleep, improved health, and even kindness.

When your mind is speeding along like a freight train full of things you need to do and remember, meditation can help you to calm down and smooth out those busy thoughts. It won't get rid of your thoughts, but it will help give you space from them so you can think more clearly. Meditation is about taking a break, being in the moment, and just breathing.

Meditation is good for both your mind and your body. It helps improve your concentration and feelings of wellbeing and positivity.

You might have heard of meditation before, or seen people doing it. Most meditation involves sitting quietly with your eyes closed and concentrating on your breathing. While you're doing this, your mind will usually start jumping from one thing to the next—this is totally normal! The aim is to let your thoughts and feelings come and go, not turn them off completely. Gradually, your heart rate will slow down and your body will relax. People who practice meditation every day find that over many months their thoughts slowly start to jump around less and less.

All around the world, people from different backgrounds, including athletes, doctors, lawyers, CEOs, parents, and kids, regularly practice meditation.

You can meditate on your own—perhaps using an app like Headspace or Smiling Mind to guide you—or with a teacher, or friend. Meditating for even a few minutes each day can make a difference, but you can do it for however long you like. Some Buddhist monks meditate for hours without taking a break! Most people who meditate only do it for about 5–10 minutes a day.

Like anything else, it takes a bit of practice to learn how to meditate. But there's no such thing as making a mistake when you're meditating!

There are many different meditation techniques. Here's a simple one to try. You might feel a bit silly at first, but don't worry—you'll soon get used to it!

DID YOU KNOW?

There's evidence that people meditated as long ago as 5000 to 3500 BCE. That's over 7,000 years ago!

ACTIVITY: MEDITATION FOR FOCUS

For this type of meditation, you're going to focus on your breath. Remember—it's okay for your mind to wander. That's what minds do! Every time you notice some new thoughts popping in, try to concentrate on your breathing again. This helps you learn to recognize when your attention has shifted, so you can let go of the distraction and re-focus.

1. Find a quiet, comfortable place where you won't be interrupted, such as your bedroom.

2. Decide how long you're going to meditate for. When you're first starting, 2 or 3 minutes is long enough. As you get better at it, you might be able to do it for 10 or even 15 minutes!

3. Find a comfortable position. This could be sitting on the edge of your bed or in a chair, with your hands resting in your lap. You could sit cross-legged on a cushion or on the floor if that's comfortable. You can even meditate lying down—as long as you're comfy and relaxed!

4. Now, close your eyes and start concentrating on your breath going in and out, your chest rising and falling. If you find yourself thinking about something funny your friend did today, the game of soccer you've got tomorrow, the homework that's due, or the pain in your knees from sitting cross-legged for too long, remind yourself to focus on your breathing—in and out.

5. Every time your mind goes on a new little adventure, just bring your attention back to your breathing. That's it!

DID YOU KNOW?

The lotus pose has been used for meditation since ancient times in India. It's kind of like sitting cross-legged, but each foot is placed up on top of the opposite thigh. It's a difficult position and requires a lot of flexibility! Can you do it?

BREATHING IS SOMETHING WE ALMOST never think about. It happens automatically! This means that many of us don't think about breathing properly. That's right—there's a proper way to breathe. When you're feeling calm, such as when you're watching TV or reading a book on your bed, your breathing and heart rate are normal. But when something unexpected and stressful happens, like you realize you've forgotten to do your homework or suddenly a volcano erupts in your living room and the floor is lava, your heart rate gets faster and your breathing becomes quick and shallow. When you do breathing exercises, you make sure you're getting enough oxygen in your bloodstream. This helps you become calm again.

TIP

At least once every day, concentrate on taking a long, deep breath.

Meditation is a good way to begin focusing on your breathing, but here are some other exercises you can try. They might help you relax after a big day, or simply when you feel like you need a bit of peace.

STOP AND SMELL THE ROSES

1. Find your favorite flower. If there isn't one growing nearby, you can imagine it. Maybe it's a luscious red rose, a velvety white gardenia, or a soft and gentle sweet pea.

2. As you smell the flower, breathing in through your nose, count to four in your head. Then stop and hold your breath for another four counts.

3. Slowly breathe out all the way through your mouth.

4. Keep smelling the flower in this way for another minute or two, or until you feel calm.

BLOW SOME BUBBLES

Find a bubble wand. Now, take a deep breath and gently blow the biggest bubble you can. If you don't have a bubble wand, close your eyes and imagine you're holding one in front of you. Take a big breath and blow an enormous, shining bubble that sparkles in the sun—the biggest bubble you can think of!

BREATHING WITH A CUDDLY COMPANION —————

Lie on your back and sit your favorite stuffed animal on your tummy. Now, start breathing and watch your toy rise up and down. If you start to laugh, Teddy gets to go on a ride!

You'll notice with this kind of breathing that your tummy grows as well as your chest. This is called breathing with your diaphragm, and it helps you relax, lowers your heart rate, and reduces stress.

GRATITUDE IS A VERY POSITIVE feeling. It can help you focus on the good things in your life and reminds you to be thankful for what you have. Think about all the things in your life that make it brighter. Doing this increases feelings of optimism, helping you feel happier each day.

You can decorate your gratitude journal with pictures of things that make you happy—photos of family and friends, pressed flowers, or drawings of happy things like the sun or a bird singing in a tree.

> **"IF YOU ARE IN A BAD MOOD, GO FOR A WALK. IF YOU ARE STILL IN A BAD MOOD, GO FOR ANOTHER WALK."**
> —HIPPOCRATES,
> THE "FATHER OF MEDICINE"

ACTIVITY: A GRATITUDE JOURNAL

In a journal or on your computer, once a day or once a week (whichever works for you!), set aside a few minutes to write down three things you're grateful for. They can be anything you like, no matter how small or big—it's totally up to you! During the day, keep an eye out for things that you're happy to have in your life so you can record them. Here are some ideas to get you started:

❀ A person you love having in your life

❀ A pet you have now or one you once had

❀ Your favorite hobby

❀ Your favorite thing in your bedroom

❀ The thing you love most about your house

❀ The body parts you're most happy you have

❀ The best vacation you ever went on

❀ A song that you love

❀ A skill that you have

❀ The food you're most thankful you get to eat

❀ A memory of the last time you laughed uncontrollably or had fun with a friend

❀ A time in your life that you're glad happened

❀ Something nice that someone did for you

❀ Something nice that someone did for someone else—it's reassuring to know that good things happen in the world

❀ A challenge you faced that you're glad you overcame

❀ Things that you're grateful aren't in your life

TIP

If you're feeling a bit down, ask yourself: "What's one thing I can do that I know will put me in a good mood?" And then find a way to do it, even if it's only for a little while. Maybe it's calling a friend or talking to a family member, going for a walk, reading a book, or dancing to a song—do the silliest, most energetic dance you can!

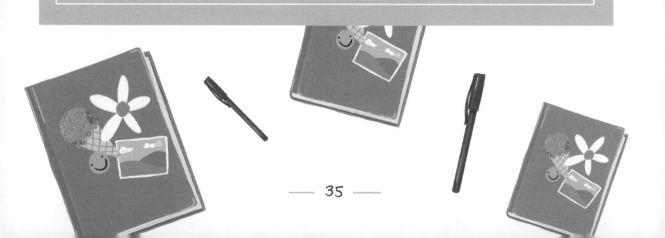

KATE BARRY
Australia

Kate has always loved beautiful hair scrunchies. Inspired by friends and family running their own businesses, she decided to create her own business called Scrunchie Munchies. Kate hopes her lovingly handmade scrunchies put a bit of magic into people's hair. She also has a range of scrunchies where 100% of the profits are donated to raise money for Australian wildlife impacted by the 2020 wildfires.

1. How old are you now and how old were you when you started Scrunchie Munchies?

I'm thirteen and I started Scrunchie Munchies when I was eleven.

2. Where did you grow up and how did that inspire you?

I've always lived in the Inner West in Sydney. From award-winning local authors, to teachers at both the schools I've been to, I've grown up around fabulous people. My mom has her own business. I've always been told that girls can do anything; you just need to work hard and persist.

3. Why did you start making scrunchies?

Back in my mom's day, scrunchies were all the rage. When scrunchies made a comeback, I was astounded by the prices. Even though the quality wasn't all that great, as a lot were mass-produced overseas, most cost over $10. Initially, I thought a scrunchie business would make some money to pay for tickets to see *Harry Potter and the Cursed Child* in Melbourne. It took off, so I built myself a website and

Scrunchie Munchies was born. My great-nanna was a dressmaker, and my mom sews. Mom helped me to master the sewing machine. It takes a while to make the tubes and then stuff them with elastic.

4. What's your favorite thing about scrunchies?

There are always new possibilities. I spend a lot of time looking at the latest fabrics to keep mixing up the range. I love coming up with new ideas. My scrunchies are stocked in the school uniform store and it's so great seeing the girls wearing my scrunchies each day.

5. What's your favorite pastime or hobby?

Reading and doing drama. I've been going to Australian Theatre for Young People since I was seven and just love to perform. At school, I'm on the Debating and Public Speaking team. Also, I love hanging out with my friends.

6. How do you stay positive when times are tough?

Turn to family and friends for advice. Play the "glad game": when you think about it, there's always something you can find to be glad about in any situation.

7. What would you say is your biggest achievement so far?

Last year I was awarded the Spirit of the Junior School award, after being at my school for only two years. I loved being the Student Representative Council Captain and working with girls of all ages. In 2019 I was also awarded a Fred Hollows Humanity Award for outstanding sixth-grade students who make a positive difference in their community.

My biggest business achievement is still running a business two years after I launched it. At times it's hard, but there's always someone new to discover my website (which I built myself). There's a real buzz when an order comes in and I send out a note of thanks.

8. Do you have any tips to help kids live on the bright side?
Believe in yourself. Everyone's different and you have to think that anything is possible. There are people to turn to when times get tough so don't forget to ask for help if you need it and keep following your dreams.

POSITIVE AND NEGATIVE THOUGHTS

OUR THOUGHTS ARE VERY POWERFUL. They can make us feel happy, sad, calm, mad, fearful, worried, excited, bored, confused, amused, and hopeful. We each have our own little voice inside us that guides us through the day. Sometimes this voice reminds us to do things; it also helps us work out what we feel like for lunch, or tells us that we look great today. But at other times, this voice can remind us of things that are bad in the world, tell us we've made a mistake or done something wrong—or that everything's ruined and it's the worst day of our life.

Even if we've had a day full of good times, if one bad thing has happened, we often tend to focus on that more than any of the nice parts of the day. Try to get into the habit of going over the good things from your day, rather than the bad things.

When you think happy thoughts, it actually impacts your body: your muscles relax and your breathing becomes deeper. But when you think about things that make you unhappy, your heart rate and breathing get faster, making you feel stressed.

It's important to remember that our thoughts are not facts. So, when you're thinking about something negative, always ask yourself: "Is it really true?" Would your friends or family think the same thing?

We should always speak about ourselves—and other people—in a positive and nice way.

WHAT'S YOUR SUPERPOWER?

EVERYONE HAS AT LEAST a few little superpowers!

Some examples are:

- ✿ The ability to spot caterpillars in the wild
- ✿ Always knowing what you want to order when you get to the front of the line
- ✿ Always knowing exactly how much ketchup you're going to need on your plate
- ✿ Never stepping on a Lego when they're lying on the living room floor
- ✿ Always replacing the toilet roll when it's empty

Or could it be that your little superpowers help the planet? Maybe you always have your reusable straws and bags handy.

Can you think of your three favorite little superpowers?

BE YOURSELF

You've probably been told many times to "just be yourself." But it takes a while to figure out who *yourself* actually is! (Plenty of adults haven't worked themselves out all that well yet either.) It's easy to feel like you have to change to fit in with other people—but it's better to learn who you are and what you enjoy doing, then be that person. You might find that who you are changes depending on who you're with, and you feel a bit different with different people. It can take time to find your people—the ones you can laugh with easily, feel comfortable doing nothing with, and who make you feel the best. Around these people, you don't have to try to be yourself—you just are.

GROWTH MINDSET

> "I HAVE NOT FAILED.
> I'VE JUST FOUND 10,000
> WAYS THAT WON'T WORK."
> —THOMAS EDISON, INVENTOR

YOU MIGHT HAVE HEARD OF a growth mindset before. It's the idea that not knowing something, or not knowing how to do something, isn't a bad thing—it's an opportunity to learn new things or get better at a skill! When we attempt something, and it doesn't work right away, it means we can approach it in a different way next time.

Our brains aren't fixed—they never stop learning, making new connections, and being rewired. That means you can teach yourself to do all kinds of things with a bit of practice. On your second go at doing something new—in fact, with each attempt—your brain will have processed everything you experienced the time before and you'll find that you've gotten better at it. The more you practice, the more you'll improve. So, if there's something you can't do yet but you'd like to, it's there for you to explore when you're ready.

For example, if you're learning the piano, and you want to be able to play a more difficult piece, start small. Learn each hand separately, one phrase at a time—and each time you try, you'll be a little bit better than you were before!

It's also important to remember to enjoy the thing you're trying to do. If you're doing something with love and joy, it won't matter how many times you have to try it as you continue to improve.

Everyone has trouble doing certain things, but we can all get better; no matter how young or old we are, we can grow a bit more each day! All of us make mistakes along the way, and that's okay. We'll do things we later regret, and that's okay too. Making mistakes is part of learning to do the right thing. Sometimes when we've done something wrong, it can feel so big and awful, as though we're underneath a cloud that's raining only on us, and like things will never be right again. But that doesn't mean that tomorrow won't bring better things. The rain will dry up, and the sun will poke through the clouds.

TIP

When you're learning something, try not to look at your results but instead focus on how much effort you've put in to doing it. Your hard work is your superpower! If you're focused on learning and having fun, the results will take care of themselves.

ACTIVITY: MAKE YOUR OWN AFFIRMATIONS

Affirmations are words of positivity and encouragement. You can give affirmations to other people, but you can also give them to yourself. Think about some nice things you think about yourself and other people. Start keeping a journal where you write down the things you love about yourself, your life and those around you. For example:

- ❁ I am smart.
- ❁ I am strong.
- ❁ I always do the best I can.
- ❁ There is no one quite like me.
- ❁ I love my family and they love me.
- ❁ I have the best friends I could ask for.
- ❁ I am proud of myself.
- ❁ If I make a mistake, that's okay.
- ❁ I live on the bright side.

FEATURED ORGANIZATION
MINDFUL SCHOOLS

Mindful Schools works with teachers and students around the United States to promote mental health and well-being in schools. Life can be stressful, and often the difficulties kids face at home negatively affect their ability to learn and grow. Mindful Schools trains teachers in techniques that help them create a peaceful and loving environment for themselves and their students.

Growing up is hard enough, but according to the National Survey of Children's Health, almost half of children in the U.S. have experienced at least one serious negative event or trauma. As a result, anxiety among children and teens is at an all-time high. Teachers are often strained, too, making it difficult for them to tend to their students' needs. That's why it's more important than ever that teachers and students be given the emotional support they need to stay curious, kind, and patient, even when times are tough.

Mindful Schools started in a classroom at Emerson Elementary School in Oakland, California, and it has since grown to serve schools all over the country. Today, more than 3 million children have been helped by this incredible program!

TIP

There's nothing like a good belly laugh to chase the gray clouds away. Be silly with your friends, or watch a funny show or video.

HAILE THOMAS
United States of America

Haile Thomas is an international speaker, wellness and compassion activist, vegan food and lifestyle influencer, chef, motivational speaker, writer, and the CEO of non-profit organization HAPPY (Happy Active Positive Purposeful Youth)— and she's only nineteen!

When she was nine years old, Haile and her four-year-old sister Nia started a YouTube channel called Kids Can Cook. Today, Haile still runs a YouTube channel where she shares lifestyle videos and vegan recipes. She has over 100,000 followers on Instagram.

Both of Haile's parents are Jamaican, but Haile was born in Dallas, Texas. Haile's mother started teaching her to cook when she was five. Later, Haile's father was diagnosed with type 2 diabetes, so she began looking for healthier ways to prepare food. Through healthy eating and better lifestyle choices, her family successfully reversed her father's diabetes. This inspired Haile to do more to educate and empower young people to look after their minds and bodies.

At the age of twelve, Haile founded HAPPY to promote youth empowerment. HAPPY's philosophy is to look after your physical health through food and exercise, your mental health through a positive mindset and self-care, and your soul through having purpose, compassion for others and good relationships. Haile wants to help others grow into the best version of themselves, encourage self-reflection, and motivate young people to live a life full of purpose.

LITTLE GOALS AND BIG GOALS

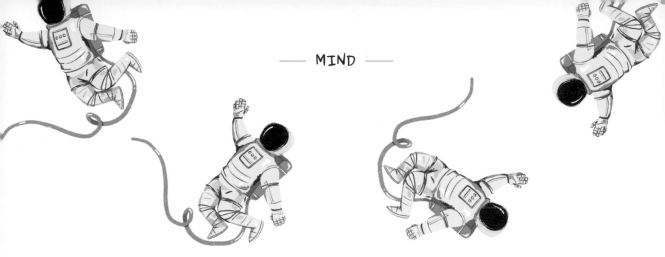

DO YOU HAVE A GOAL, or something you want to be able to do? This might be something huge, like maybe one day you want to become an astronaut and go to the moon. Perhaps it's learning to play a piece on the violin or cello. Or maybe it's something smaller, like finishing your homework by tomorrow. Whatever your goals, it's worth having a plan to help you achieve them.

Whether your goals are big or small, try to break them down into smaller, more achievable steps. For example, if you want to walk 10 miles in a week, try walking for 1 mile each weekday, then 2.5 miles on Saturday and Sunday.

Maybe you have three pages of math homework to do by tomorrow and it's 4 p.m. Say it takes 10 minutes to complete each page. Aim to do your first page by 4:10 p.m., then take a five minute break before tackling the next page. In 45 minutes, you'll be done!

It's also good to reward yourself when you achieve each of your little goals, not just your final goal. Have a small treat ready for your five-minute break, such as a piece of chocolate, a delicious drink, reading a chapter of your book, or stepping outside to look at the sky. When you've reached your final goal, give yourself a bigger reward, such as an episode of a TV show, a level of your favorite video game, or a trip to the park.

MIND GAME:
I PACKED MY BAG

Memory games make our brains stronger and smarter, and can improve our focus and concentration. They're also a fun way to practice mindfulness, because you become fully focused on playing. "I packed my bag" is an old favorite. It's perfect for passing the time when you're traveling somewhere in the car, while you're lying outside in the grass on a sunny day making daisy chains, or jumping on the trampoline.

You need at least two people to play. The first player says, "I packed my bag with a . . ." and chooses an object, like a toothbrush. The next player then has to say, "I packed my bag with a toothbrush and a . . ." and adds another object to the list, like a book. With each turn, the list gets longer. Each player has to recite the whole list in order and then add something new to it. As soon as someone forgets something, they're out of the game. The last player left who can remember everything is the winner!

You can pack all kinds of silly things. There's always room in your bag for an elephant!

BODY

TO FEEL GOOD EVERY DAY, it's important to look after your body. This involves moving around, exercising, and stretching. Did you know that there are ways you can move your body that also make your mind feel good, including how you stand and games you can play? This chapter is all about fun ways to get moving!

DID YOU KNOW?

When you exercise, your body releases chemicals called endorphins, which create positive feelings and a better outlook on life.

GET ACTIVE

EXERCISE ISN'T ONLY GOOD FOR YOUR PHYSICAL HEALTH:

people who exercise regularly also have a more positive mood. Exercising for as little as 30 minutes can make you feel less worried and help you sleep better. Regular exercise gives you stronger bones and muscles, plus your heart will be healthier—something that makes everyone feel great!

If you're after something to quickly boost your mood, try getting out and going for a run.

Here are some other types of exercise you could try:

- ✿ Bike riding or scootering
- ✿ Dancing
- ✿ Swimming
- ✿ Walking
- ✿ Sports
- ✿ Skipping rope
- ✿ Playing hide and seek
- ✿ Yoga
- ✿ Gardening
- ✿ Housework. Yep—vacuuming is good for your mood *and* makes your parents happy!

"WHEN YOU HAVE A DREAM YOU HAVE TO WORK HARD TO ACHIEVE THAT DREAM. YOUR DREAMS WHEN YOU ARE YOUNG CAN BE THE FORCE THAT KEEPS YOU GOING."

—EVONNE GOOLAGONG CAWLEY, AUSTRALIAN TENNIS PLAYER

TIP

Find a form of exercise you enjoy, so you'll be more likely to stick to it and want to do it every day. For example, you might prefer swimming over running, or riding your bike over doing push-ups.

SUPERHERO WORKOUT PLAN

DO THESE EXERCISES EACH DAY and you'll be ready for anything! If you find it difficult at first, try doing them every second or third day to begin with. Gradually, you'll build up your strength.

✿ 10 star jumps

✿ 10 push-ups

✿ 10 lunges

✿ 10 squats

✿ Balance for 15 seconds on one foot, then do the same on the other one.

✿ Jog in place for 10 seconds—pretend you're chasing someone!

✿ Jump as high as you can 5 times—try to touch the ceiling!

✿ Crawl along the floor like you're Spiderman climbing up a wall.

✿ Jump forward as far as you can, as though you're leaping from one building to another.

✿ Plank for 30 seconds—you're lying low, ready to jump up at any minute!

✿ Plant your feet on the ground and punch the air repeatedly, first with one fist then with the other. Look at those moves!

TIP

Lower your shoulders—go on; do it right now! When we feel tense, our shoulders go upward toward our ears. When you lower them, you'll feel more relaxed!

COCO GAUFF
United States of America

Cori "Coco" Gauff is an eighteen-year-old professional tennis player. When she was little, Coco took part in lots of different sports, including basketball and track and field. Inspired by her idols Serena and Venus Williams, she decided to try tennis. She turned out to be so good at it that she was given a sponsorship to train at an academy in France.

When she was fifteen, Coco won her very first professional singles tournament. Then she became the youngest player ever to qualify for the main draw at Wimbledon. At the time of this writing, Coco is the youngest tennis player ranked in the women's top 100.

In an Instagram post for Behind the Racket—a site where professional tennis players share their personal stories—Coco talked about the pressure she felt to always be "the youngest to do things." She also revealed that for a while she doubted whether tennis was what she really wanted to do. Suddenly, she found herself not enjoying what she'd previously loved—which was playing tennis! For about a year, Coco felt very depressed. "When you are in that dark mindset you don't look on the bright side of things too often, which is the hardest part." She said she spent many moments "sitting, thinking, and crying."

Happily, Coco began to get to know herself better and realized that she needed to start playing tennis for herself and not for other people. Her love of playing tennis returned and she was able to come back stronger.

Coco describes herself as "just a kid who has some pretty big dreams." After beating world number four Naomi Osaka at the Australian Open in 2020, Coco mentioned that she had some homework due. Luckily, her teachers were letting her submit some assignments late, so she was looking forward to catching up on some sleep!

Above all, Coco's story shows how important it is to do the things you love for yourself, and no one else!

LORENA RAMÍREZ
Mexico

María Lorena Ramírez Hernández ("Lorena" for short) is a Rarámuri runner who grew up scaling the vast canyons and walking miles across the rocky landscape of Sierra Tarahumara in Chihuahua, Mexico. The Rarámuri are a group of indigenous people whose name means "light-footed people" or "those who run fast." Lorena, who used to herd sheep, proved that she has an amazing ability to run great distances without tiring, winning her first ultramarathon in 2017 at the Ultra Trail Cerro Rojo, a 50-kilometer race in the mountains, and placing fifth in the women's category in the 2018 Tenerife Trail, a 63-mile trail located in the Canary Islands. She has also finished first and second in 100-kilometer ultramarathons.

Not only are these feats impressive due to the sheer distances and tough terrains of the races but also because Lorena competes without any formal training or fancy sports equipment. She proudly races wearing her traditional skirt and huarache sandals—representing her Rarámuri heritage through her clothing. Lorena has been described as serious and shy, but as the first Rarámuri woman to race in an ultramarathon in Europe and running against elite competitors from many different countries, she is bringing international attention to her indigenous community. Her father, grandfather, and several of her eight brothers and sisters run too.

When Lorena isn't running ultramarathons and breaking stereotypes, she spreads awareness and knowledge about Tarahumara and Mexican culture and people.

YOGA

YOGA COMBINES BREATHING TECHNIQUES AND meditation with exercise, making it good for both your mind and your body. It's also an approach to life that focuses on peace and harmony. Plus, all you need to get started is yourself!

Yoga techniques include things such as postures (poses, or positions, that you hold for several seconds or more), movement and stretches, breathing exercises, and relaxation. Many thousands of years ago, people in India called yogis developed the yoga poses, or "asanas." The yogis were inspired by animals and plants, which you can often see in the names of the poses. Each pose is designed to improve flexibility, strength, balance, focus, and inner peace. Regular yoga practice is thought to ease some symptoms of stress-related medical conditions.

Here are a few popular animal poses to try. Some people are more naturally bendy than others, so just do what feels comfortable for you. In each pose, breathe through your nose slowly, deeply, and calmly. If you feel the urge, let out your animal noises!

THE PURR-FECT CAT POSE

The cat pose is great for your back and will strengthen your arms and tummy! Place your hands and knees on the floor, with your wrists positioned under your shoulders and your knees underneath your hips. Your back should look like a table top. Now, tuck in your belly toward your spine. Breathe in through your nose. Then, as you breathe out, bring your chin into your chest and arch your back like a cat. Hold the pose for five seconds, then return to the initial position. Meow! Repeat five times, breathing in and out slowly and deeply.

MOOOVE LIKE A COW

From your cat pose, you can move into the cow pose. This pose is great for making your spine more flexible and stretching your back.

Keep your hands and knees on the ground, with your wrists underneath your shoulders and your knees underneath your hips. Breathe in slowly as you move from your arched cat pose, push your bellybutton downward toward the floor and raise your face so you're looking straight ahead. Hold the pose for five seconds. Then, as you move back into your cat pose, you can breathe out and let out a big MOOOO!

STRETCH LIKE A DOWNWARD DOG

From your position on your hands and knees, it's time to embrace your inner pooch. This pose strengthens your upper body and lower body and stretches you out at the same time!

Move your hands forward one hand's length, curl your toes under, and push your hips up to the sky. To give your leg muscles and hamstrings a stronger stretch, push your heels a little closer to the floor. Woof!

LET'S GECKO-ING ON THIS LIZARD POSE ————————

This funky lizard lunge needs a bit of flexibility, but it's great for your hips. From your downward dog pose, move your body forward slightly so your shoulders are above your wrists. Then place your right foot just to the right of your right hand, next to your pinkie finger. Make sure your right knee is above your heel, not in front of it.

For a deeper stretch, try dropping your elbows so your forearms are on the ground, if you can. Never force your body. Some bodies are loose and bendy, while other bodies are pretty tight. Yoga suits everyone, but you only need to do what feels good for you! Now switch sides and bring your left foot forward.

DON'T FROGET THE FROG POSE ————

You might already know this one if you've ever played leapfrog. This pose opens your hip joints.

Come down into a squat, knees apart, with your hands on the ground in front of you. Say "Ribbit, ribbit!" Sometimes you can't help hopping around the room!

THE ROARSOME LION POSE

Start on your hands and knees, move your bottom back to your heels and get ready for your pounce. Move forward onto your knees again, stick out your tongue and let out your scariest ROAR! This strengthens your lungs, throat, and voice, and can also help you let out your frustrations.

SSSSTRETCH LIKE A COBRA

Imagine you have no legs! Lie on your stomach, face down, with your palms resting gently on the ground on either side of your head. Squeeze your abs (your abdominal or tummy muscles) to help you lift your head, shoulders, and maybe your chest off the ground, moving slowly and gently.

This pose has lots of benefits, including strengthening your spine and shoulders, and improving digestion. Cobras are famous for being able to lift their heads way up off the ground. The king cobra can even lift itself high enough that it can look an adult in the eye! But be careful not to overdo it. This pose can cause back pain if not practiced safely. Remember to keep your tummy muscles engaged, as this will help protect your lower back.

CHILD'S POSE

Children are animals too! This is a good pose to move into after the cobra pose to relax and help the circulation in your back.

Kneel on something soft, like a yoga mat, towel, or carpet. With your big toes touching and your knees apart, stretch forward onto the mat with your arms either by your side or extended over your head. Rest your forehead on the ground and breathe in and out, slowly and deeply.

THE TALLEST TREE

Trees are important for animals: they provide shelter and homes for small creatures in their hollows. The tree pose strengthens your ankles and calves and helps improve your balance. Stand on one leg, place the sole of your other foot on your inner thigh or on the muscle below your knee, and put your palms together in front of you. If you need help balancing, try focusing on one point a couple of feet in front of you. Now, imagine you're a giant oak tree, hundreds of years old, your roots growing deep into the ground from the bottom of your foot. Maybe you have an owl nesting on your shoulder! For an even taller tree, raise your arms above your head, keeping your palms together.

What's your favorite animal? What do you think its yoga pose would look like?

THE PIRATE STANCE

If you're feeling a bit down in the dumps and nothing seems to be going your way, channel your inner pirate. Jump into action, put your hands on your hips, legs apart, and shoulders back. Throw up your arm like you're holding a sword and shout, "Avast!"

Some other pirate sayings to try are:

- ✿ "Ahoy, landlubber!," "Ahoy, me hearties!," or "Ahoy, matey!"
- ✿ "Aye aye, Cap'n!"
- ✿ "Shiver me timbers!"
- ✿ "Yo ho ho!"
- ✿ "Ye scurvy dog!"
- ✿ "Thar she blows!"
- ✿ "Sail, ho!"
- ✿ "Land, ho!" (Put your hand above your eyes to block the sun's glare as you stare out across the sea.)

SLEEP TIGHT

GETTING ENOUGH SLEEP IS ONE of the best things you can do for both your body and your mind. Sleep gives our bodies a chance to rest and repair. It also lets our brains organize our thoughts and emotions and even solve problems for us! When we don't get enough sleep, we can become cranky and clumsy and have trouble remembering things. And if our sleep is bad for long stretches of time, we can not recover well from illness or injury and even start hallucinating!

People of different ages need different amounts of sleep. Babies sleep the most—around 14 hours a day! Kids need about 10 hours, and adults need at least 7 or 8 hours a night. But lots of people find it difficult to get the full amount.

Sleeping well actually takes practice, so be patient!

Getting good sleep has a lot to do with how well you prepare. Because you need to put your mind to sleep as well as your body, calming down is an important part of getting ready for bed. Check out these tips for getting quality ZZZs.

- ✿ Try to go to bed at the same time every night. You'll sleep better if you stick to a routine.
- ✿ If you can, avoid looking at screens—like a phone, TV, or iPad—for at least one hour before bed.

✿ In the evening, avoid food and drinks that contain a lot of sugar or caffeine, such as soft drinks, iced tea, and chocolate.

✿ Come up with a soothing bedtime routine. Here are some things you can do to relax before bed:

- Take a warm bath or shower.

- Put on some comfy pajamas.

- Read a book.

- Drink a cup of chamomile tea or warm milk and have a light bedtime snack.

- Meditate or do some breathing exercises.

- Turn off the main lights and turn on a lamp instead.

- Write in your journal.

- Do some coloring or draw a picture.

- Listen to peaceful music.

✿ Exercise during the day, not in the evening or after dinner.

✿ Try not to do homework on your bed, otherwise you might associate your bed with working instead of sleeping!

✿ The ideal sleeping conditions are dark, cool, and quiet. It's more difficult to sleep when you're too hot.

✿ When you're in bed, get into a comfortable position and try to keep still, even if you feel restless. Pretending to be asleep can actually help you fall asleep!

✿ Try not to sleep in too late, even on the weekend, because then at night you won't be tired and you'll have trouble sticking to your bedtime routine.

✿ If your mind is buzzing with thoughts and you're having trouble getting to sleep, try telling yourself a happy story in your mind. Just start with "Once upon a time" and go from there.

FUN FACTS ABOUT SLEEP ————————————

- ✿ Humans spend about one third of their lives asleep. That's about 25 years!

- ✿ Sleep is just as important as nutrition and exercise. In fact, you'll die more quickly from a lack of sleep than a lack of food.

- ✿ It's normal to wake up briefly several times during the night—though hardly anyone remembers this by morning. The waking, or coming back to consciousness—similar to a diver swimming up to the surface—happens because people have sleep cycles of about 90 minutes.

- ✿ People are taller in the morning! When you're lying down, the discs in your spine spread out. But when you're up and about, they get squashed back together again.

FUN AND GAMES

THERE ARE LOTS OF GAMES you can play that help you move your body and have lots of fun at the same time! Getting in the zone when you're playing a game is the funnest form of mindfulness. You might already know some of the games described on these pages, but maybe there are a few new ones that you haven't tried yet.

STUCK IN THE MUD

This is a good game for six or more people. Work out a boundary area, then decide who's going to be "it." The person who's "it" has to chase all the other players around and try to tag as many people as they can. When they catch someone, that person is stuck in the mud! The stuck person then has to stand still with their legs apart and can only become free again if another player crawls between their legs. The game continues until everyone is stuck.

WHAT TIME IS IT, MR. WOLF?

Choose one person to be Mr. Wolf. This person stands at one end of the playing area, while all the other players stand at the other end, about 30 feet away. Mr. Wolf then turns his back. The players at the other end call out, "What time is it, Mr. Wolf?" and Mr. Wolf has to answer with the time (keeping his back turned). Whatever time he answers—1 o'clock, 6 o'clock, 10 o'clock—the players have to take that number of steps toward Mr. Wolf (for 10 o'clock, for instance, they take ten steps). Each time the players ask, "What time is it, Mr. Wolf?," and Mr. Wolf answers, they take more steps and get closer and closer. When Mr. Wolf feels like it, instead of answering with the time, he can shout, "It's dinnertime!," and turn around and chase the players back toward the starting line. Whoever he catches first has to be Mr. Wolf for the next game. If he catches no one, he has to be Mr. Wolf again.

SPOOKY SARDINES

This works best with at least four people.

To make this game the spookiest it can be, you'll want to play at nighttime! One person runs and hides somewhere in the house, while the rest of the players count to 30, then they all spread out to look for the person who's hiding. When one player finds the person hiding, instead of letting everyone else know, they climb into the hiding spot too! As each player finds the people hiding and joins them, they all end up squashed together like sardines. The last person to find the group has to be the first to hide in the next game.

JUMP THE BROOM

This game is suitable for any number of players. Place a broom so it's lying down flat on a soft area of grass outside. Each player takes a turn standing away from the broom and spinning around until they're dizzy—up to 20 times. Then they approach the broom and try to jump over it without falling.

RACES

There are lots of different types of races you can try. Pick a start and finish line, then decide on how you're going to race: hopping on one leg, crawling, running backward, the sideways crab walk, or wheelbarrow-style with two people on each team and one holding the other up by their legs while the "wheelbarrow" walks along on their hands!

BALL GAMES

Simply find a ball, go outside, and play. You could catch or bounce a basketball, hit a tennis ball back and forth with a friend or against a wall (no tennis court needed), or kick a ball around!

THE LAUGHING GAME

Gather together your funniest friends for this game—and make sure you play outside! Give each person a cup of water, and when you say "Go!," everyone fills their mouth with water. The aim is to make all the others laugh while trying not to laugh yourself. The last person with water still in their mouth is the winner. Laughter is the best medicine!

RED LIGHT, GREEN LIGHT

Choose one person to be "it"—this person is the traffic light. The other players stand in a group at the starting line, about 30 feet away. The person who's "it" turns their back to the players. When "it" calls "Green light," the players move toward them until "it" shouts, "Red light" and spins around. All the players must freeze instantly. If "it" catches any of the players still moving, that player must return to the starting line. "It" then returns to their starting position and says "Green light" so the players can begin moving again until the next "Red light" is called. If a player manages to tag "it," they become "it" for the next game.

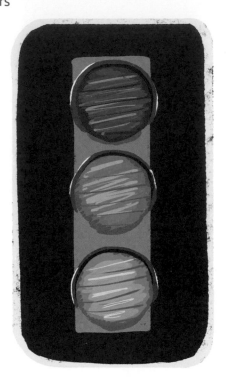

To add a challenge, at the beginning of the game decide on a particular way the players have to move—for example, hopping, walking backward, or crawling. You could also introduce a "Yellow light": as soon as they hear these words, players have to move in slow motion.

JUGGLING

If you're looking for an activity to do on your own, juggling is a great skill to learn. There are lots of instructional videos online. All you need are a few balls of the same size that you can hold easily in your hand—hacky sacks are perfect for juggling!

TIP

Try to smile, even when you don't feel like it. We smile when we feel happy, but smiling can also make us happy!

THE GREAT OUTDOORS

BEING IN NATURE MAKES US happy. Spending time outdoors under the sky, surrounded by trees, feeling the sunshine on our skin, the breeze in our hair and the soft grass under our feet has a big impact on our brains. Our anxiety and stress reduce, and our creativity increases. Being in nature is even thought to make us kinder!

Here are some ways you might like to get outside. There are also some ideas here for you to continue practicing mindfulness.

GETTING OUTSIDE

GO ON A STAR WALK ——————————————

The night sky is filled with wonders. You can go on a star walk, or just sit or lie in the grass—as long as you can see the sky. The higher you are, the clearer the sky will be, so if there's a hill nearby, climb it! Also, you'll be able to see the planets and constellations better when you're away from houses and streetlights, so ask an adult to take you to an area beyond the city lights. You might want to keep an eye on the moon cycle too so you can go out when it's darkest. The darker it is, the longer it can take your eyes to adjust— up to half an hour!

Depending on where you are in the world, the time of year, and how much light pollution there is, the things you see in the sky will change. You can make a star journal to keep track of what you find.

Here are some famous constellations to look for in North America, or you can use your imagination and find your own formations hidden in the stars.

- ✿ The Northern Cross
- ✿ Orion
- ✿ Canis Major
- ✿ The North Star
- ✿ The Big Dipper and the Little Dipper

There are plenty of great star-watching resources available. Download an app, such as SkyView Lite or Star Walk 2; search the web for a star chart; or find out the dates for meteor showers, when there'll be more than the usual number of shooting stars streaking through the sky.

DID YOU KNOW?

The brightest stars aren't always stars! To spot the planet Venus, look for the brightest light in the night sky after the Moon. Venus has two nicknames: the Morning Star and the Evening Star. Because it's always relatively close to the sun, you'll always spot Venus near the horizon. In the morning, it will rise a few hours before the sun, while in the evening it will be the first object to appear shortly after the sun sets—when the sky becomes just dark enough.

WATCH THE CLOUDS

On a lovely warm day when the sky is full of fluffy white clouds, take a blanket and lie down outside (or just lie on the grass!). Stare up at the sky and you'll see the clouds moving slowly or quickly. Are they fluffy like cotton, wispy and feathery, or huge and heavy looking? Do they look like you could walk on them, or would you fall right through? Are they changing shape or staying the same? If it's evening, they might even be changing color!

Now, see if you can find anything in the clouds. Maybe there are shapes, like a heart. There might be a big fire-breathing dragon, a person's face, or an animal, such as an elephant with a long trunk, a round and cuddly koala, or a rabbit with a fluffy tail. If you're with a friend, take turns explaining what you've found in the clouds. Can you see what each other sees?

DID YOU KNOW?

There are lots of different types of clouds you can use for cloud watching, but the best kind are called cumulus clouds. These are big, sit low in the sky, and have a puffy cotton-wool appearance, often with flat bottoms.

LIE UNDER A TREE

Take some time to lie under a tree and look up at the light dancing through the leaves. Feel the softness of the breeze and the tender green grass or clover growing around you.

HUG A TREE

Choose a tree that's large enough to wrap your arms around and give it a hug. Feel its cool trunk and the texture of its bark. Is it papery and rough, or silky, soft, and smooth? Did you know that hugging trees has a positive effect on wellbeing? Tree-hugging has been shown to soothe us, make us feel calmer, and give us a sense of comfort.

In Japan, they practice *shinrin-yoku*, which means "forest bathing." This is a feeling of soaking in the atmosphere of the forest, and connecting with the trees through sight, smell, hearing, touch, and taste.

Trees are our friends. You can even talk to them if you want; they're good listeners!

Do you have a favorite tree to hug?

GO FOR A WALK IN THE RAIN

Most people hate the idea of going outside when it's raining. But rain walks can be lots of fun! Put on some old clothes and sneakers—or go barefoot if you're planning to wander around your backyard—then step outside and feel the rain on your skin. It might make you shudder at first, but once your clothes are soaked, it feels great. Keep moving to make sure your body doesn't get too cold, and when you go back inside you can take a lovely hot shower or bath to warm up. Afterward, when you're warm and dressed in clean, dry clothes, you'll feel super snug and cozy.

DAISY CHAINS

In the springtime, when you're lying outside, make daisy chains. You can also use dandelions or clover flowers if they're big enough. Find the flowers with the juiciest stems, create a thin slit in the stem with your thumbnail, then thread the stem of the next flower through the hole. Continue making holes and threading on new flowers until you have a chain.

GO ON A PICNIC

You don't have to go anywhere special to have a lovely picnic. Take some yummy food and a blanket to a nearby park, your own backyard, or even just your balcony. As long as there's shade, sunshine, and you can see the sky, you can have an outdoor lunch or snack. If it's a rainy day, why not sit indoors near the window and watch the rain falling outside? It's nice to be wrapped in a blanket when there's thunder rolling across the sky.

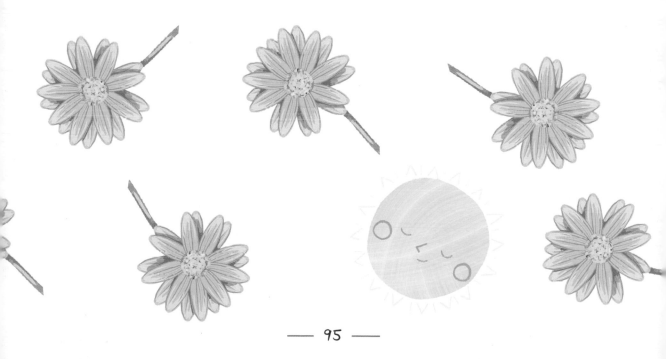

GO BIRDWATCHING

Regardless of what's happening with us humans, birds go about their business as though all is well. It can be both calming and fascinating to watch them. Find out the names of the birds in your area, plus the details of what they look like and sound like. You might be surprised at how many species of bird are in your neighborhood! Use binoculars if you have them, but you can notice a lot by sitting at a window, in your backyard, in a city green space, or in a national park. If you do venture farther from home, put on some sunscreen and pack a bottle of water and some snacks!

Remember to listen—birds are often much easier to hear than they are to see! Maybe you can even imitate the sounds they make.

DID YOU KNOW?

You can attract new birds to your yard by providing water and places where they can find shelter. When you put out water, make sure it's shallow so even small birds can stand in it to clean their feathers. If you have a birdbath, replace the water regularly to keep it fresh. Grow native grasses, flowers, shrubs, and trees in your garden so your feathered friends are supplied with shelter, nesting materials, and nectar.

SCAVENGER HUNT

Get your friends together and go on a nature-themed scavenger hunt. You can do this in a park, or in your own backyard. Here's a list of items to look for—see how many you can find. Or you could make your own list!

- ✿ Two different-colored flowers
- ✿ One spider's web
- ✿ Your favorite leaf
- ✿ A green leaf
- ✿ A brown leaf
- ✿ Two insects
- ✿ Tree bark
- ✿ Water
- ✿ One feather
- ✿ A cool rock
- ✿ Something you think could be treasure

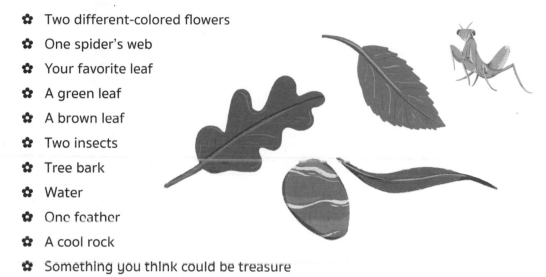

If you like, you can also take pencils and a sketchpad and draw each of the things you find.

A BOAT RACE

After it's been raining heavily, there's bound to be a stream of water running somewhere. Find some tiny boats—choose leaves or small sticks—and race them. If you live near a quiet street on a hill, sometimes there'll be enough water running by the side of the road for your boats to race. If there's a nearby bridge with water beneath it, you could race your boats under the bridge. Which one comes out the other side first? If there are cars around or the water is deep, make sure you have an adult to supervise.

MUD PIES

There's nothing better than the feeling of smooth, cool mud and watching it squeeze between your fingers. Take off your shoes, put on some old clothes. Choose a spot outside—preferably somewhere in the shade, so you can play for longer. Dig a small hole in the dirt. Place the dirt in a bucket, then all you need to do is slowly add water and it will become mud! Use old bowls or cooking utensils to make a fabulous mud pie. Decorate it with things you find outside, such as rocks, pebbles, sticks, leaves, grass, flowers, or feathers. Get creative with your pie! Then ask your family if they want to try it.

MAKE A FORT

Find the perfect place outside for a secret headquarters or clubhouse. For building materials, you could use cardboard boxes, sticks, leaves to cover and decorate your fort, a laundry basket, chairs, an outdoor table—or anything else you can think of. Make sure there's a secret password for entry!

KEEP OUT

"I TOOK A WALK IN THE WOODS AND CAME OUT TALLER THAN THE TREES."
—HENRY DAVID THOREAU, AMERICAN ESSAYIST, POET, AND PHILOSOPHER

WALKING AND HIKING AND ADVENTURING

Research any state parks and walking trails near your house, and encourage your parents to go on a weekend walking adventure with you! You could also incorporate camping, fishing, kayaking, boating, or river swimming into your adventure.

SIMBA
China

When Simba was one and a half years old, his father, Xu Chenghua, began taking him on adventures to see the world. They went on lots of day trips, and even spent eight days camping. When Xu saw his son gazing at a big blue lake one day, he knew that Simba was experiencing the beauty of nature, even though the boy was not yet able to talk. Simba's first experience seeing an elephant wasn't at a zoo, but in a forest in Laos, where the elephants were eating grass in their natural habitat.

Simba began to talk at age two and a half, and the first thing he said was: "I want to see polar bears." So, his parents took him on a six-month-long adventure through Southeast and West Asia. On a three-wheeled motorcycle, they traveled through twelve countries, eventually reaching the Arctic Circle in Russia.

When Simba was four years old, they set off again, this time on a four-month journey that took them across South America all the way to Antarctica. This made Simba the youngest Chinese person ever to set foot on both the South and North poles. On one of their adventures, Simba and his father found themselves zip-lining across a canyon to reach a waterfall in winds so strong that even Xu became scared. Simba remained calm, although after they reached safety, he admitted that he had been a little scared too.

More than anything, Simba's parents want him to be happy. His father, Xu, said: "Most kids will learn about this world and learn words through cartoon books or television, but we think it's better for our son to touch this beautiful planet with his hands and see it with his eyes."

THERE ARE SO MANY WAYS TO GET OUTSIDE

Here are some more ideas, but maybe you can think of others!

- ✿ Fly a kite (you could even try making your own kite).
- ✿ Check out your local skate park.
- ✿ Watch the sunrise or the sunset.
- ✿ Take your shoes off and walk barefoot on the grass. The grass will massage your feet!
- ✿ Become a geologist and start collecting and identifying rocks, from granite to shale to basalt.
- ✿ Walk the dog.
- ✿ In summer, have a watergun fight.
- ✿ Plant an edible garden.
- ✿ Visit your local plant nursery.
- ✿ Camp out in your backyard one night.
- ✿ Make a birdhouse.
- ✿ Play hopscotch.
- ✿ Go horseback riding.
- ✿ Bring the great outdoors indoors with nature craft.
- ✿ Go swimming in a pool, river, lake, or a blow-up pool.
- ✿ Explore whatever nature is nearby: waterfalls, caves, deserts, beaches, forests, rivers, streams, lakes, mountains, meadows, parks, and gardens.

CREATE

WHEN YOU CREATE THINGS, YOU add something new to the world. It doesn't matter how big or small your project is, making something new out of other materials is a wonderful feeling. Everything you make is an achievement!

Trying out different forms of creativity can also help you find hobbies you're interested in that you might not have known about before. Creative people are curious and they enjoy experimenting. The more things you try, the more creative you become!

And remember, if something doesn't turn out exactly as you'd hoped, it will still be something you have made, something that's special to you and that only you could have done. Next time, you can try doing it a bit differently!

DID YOU KNOW?

The shower is the perfect place for creative inspiration to strike—72% of people have creative ideas while in the shower! Letting your mind wander helps your brain have important new insights. Other good times to have creative ideas include when you're daydreaming, going for a walk, traveling somewhere in a car or on a train, bus, or plane, and even sitting on the toilet!

DRAW

DRAWING IS LOTS OF FUN, and all you need to get started is a pencil and paper. You can draw absolutely anything!

Make a hand-drawn birthday card for someone in your family or a friend as a special surprise. Pick something in your house and draw it. Do you have a fruit bowl? Or a pet? Draw your family members or your friends! Find your own unique drawing style. Do you prefer drawing people, animals, or objects?

ACTIVITY 1:
THE "GUESS WHAT I DREW" GAME

This game can make you look at ordinary things in your house that you see every day in a completely new way!

What you'll need: Paper and a pencil for each person playing
What to do: Make sure everyone has a piece of paper and a pencil. Set a timer for 10 minutes. Right away, the players each run to a different part of the house, choose something—anything from a person or pet to a piece of furniture or a toy—and draw it before the 10 minutes is up. As soon as the time's up, everyone gathers together and takes turns showing their drawings. The others try to guess what the drawing is of and find its whereabouts in the house.

ACTIVITY 2: DRAWING TUTORIALS AND LESSONS

Look up drawing tutorials on YouTube, or find some step-by-step drawing instructions like this one:

"OTHERS HAVE SEEN WHAT IS AND ASKED WHY. I HAVE SEEN WHAT COULD BE AND ASKED WHY NOT."
—PABLO PICASSO, SPANISH PAINTER

ACTIVITY 3:
DRAW YOUR HAPPY PLACE

Get some paper and every colored pencil you can find. You can use paints if you'd prefer. Sit for a moment and think of the times when you feel your happiest or most relaxed. Maybe they're when you're playing a game with your friends or family, swimming in the pool, building a sandcastle at the beach, reading a book in bed, or watching your favorite show under a blanket in the winter. Choose one of these times and do a drawing of it. Then, whenever you're feeling down, you can look at it and be reminded of this happy moment.

TIP

Go on a weekend trip to an art gallery or museum. Take along your sketchpad and see if you can recreate your favorite piece.

AELITA ANDRE
Australia

As a baby, Aelita Andre had an amazing talent for painting. When she had her first solo exhibition—in Australia, at age two—she became the world's youngest painter. Since then, Aelita's work has been exhibited in many countries. She has a big following of fans and collectors.

1. How old are you now and when did you start painting?
I'm thirteen. When I was nine months old, I crawled onto a blank canvas that my dad had prepared for himself. I started to squeeze the colorful tubes of paint and paint my first abstract painting.

2. What has inspired you?
Nature. The textures of Australian nature inspire me with their raw expressive power. I grew up in Melbourne, Australia, living next to a large nature preserve. When we traveled to central Australia, I loved the endless red sand and the wide, open skies. It was quiet and desolate yet ancient and awe-inspiring, which has influenced the style of my paintings—each canvas is like a puzzle piece of an ancient other-dimensional land.

3. What is your earliest memory of making art?
Sitting on the floor in the family room painting in a pink onesie.
I was about two. I've still got this outfit.
My mom archives all my painting clothing.

4. Tell us about your art and what it means to you.

I paint abstract paintings with all types of acrylic paints, and I add violins, toys, dinosaurs, and household objects to the canvas. An important part of my paintings is sound. I've created many "soundpaintings"—paintings which feature violins and a sound-producing painting surface. Touching it generates an atmospheric soundscape. I also love to draw realistic figurative drawings on paper, especially of horses, wolves, and fantasy creatures, and I spend many hours drawing mythical fantasy art on my iPad. One day, I'd like to turn this art into an animated feature film. To me, each painting is a window into a much greater, magical world.

5. What do you love most about painting?

It allows me to create amazing positive feelings that overcome any negative emotions—in me and the people who view my paintings. Each painting is the creation of an infinite universe. It radiates a positive energy and shines with a positive inner light. I hope the pure positivity of my paintings replaces any negative feelings and fills people with an uplifting mood and a feeling of inspiration.

6. How do you stay positive when times are tough?

Expressing my emotions artistically on the canvas keeps me positive. So does creating colorful lush fantasy drawings. I love developing and writing stories about the different magical creatures that I create in my imagination. I also listen to music and think about all the good things in my life.

7. **What would you say is your biggest achievement so far?**

My major solo exhibition in the Russian Academy of Fine Arts Museum, in the heart of Saint Petersburg, Russia, when I was nine. It was amazing to have my paintings hanging in such a prestigious place among works by some of the greatest classical painters ever.

8. **Do you have any tips to help kids live on the bright side?**

It's through your personal creativity that you become genuinely happy and more positive about life. Make a list of all the ways you can be creative, like learning a musical instrument, drawing, painting, and writing stories or poetry. If you're a more technical person, learn coding or try to think of an app to develop.

COOKING IS A FUN, CREATIVE, and often calming pastime. You'll find some brain-food recipes later in this book that you can make, but there are literally millions of other things you could cook. With a whole world of different cuisines to try, ingredients to use, and chefs to learn from, it's no wonder food is such a popular topic. There are books, TV shows, websites, apps, and Instagram pages that you can research. Or, if you're feeling brave, you could even try inventing a new dish yourself.

DID YOU KNOW?

Researchers are still discovering new things about our tastebuds, but we do know that most people can change their taste preferences. Kids actually have more tastebuds than adults, so often they're more sensitive to tastes, especially bitter ones. Expanding what foods we like makes the world around us more colorful and interesting. If you're a bit of a picky eater, or if you just want to learn to like a couple of new foods, there are some things you can do!

- Keep trying—don't give up on something if you don't like it right away! We need to try something at least 15 times before we get used to it and start to enjoy it.

- Mix food you don't like with food that you do like. For example, if you don't like zucchini, try grating some cheese on it.

- If you don't like something that's cooked one way —for example, boiled brussels sprouts—try them a different way, like brussels sprouts pan-fried in butter, with onion and bacon bits.

- Learn to associate food with good memories. If you don't like tomatoes, next time you're on vacation, try eating tomatoes. Then when you eat tomatoes again, you'll always be reminded of being on vacation!

A FEW COOKING BASICS

- ✿ Always wash your hands before cooking, and wash them often as you cook, especially if using raw meat and poultry.
- ✿ Always wash fresh fruit and vegetables before using them.
- ✿ Use different chopping boards for meat and vegetables.
- ✿ Remember to pre-heat the oven before baking.

QUICK RECIPE IDEAS

- ✿ Stewed apples with cinnamon, vanilla, and brown sugar
- ✿ Baked potatoes with sour cream, parsley, and chives
- ✿ Tomato, basil, and mozzarella salad with an olive oil, honey, and balsamic vinegar dressing
- ✿ Chicken or pork kebabs with pineapple, peppers, mushrooms, and onion
- ✿ Pasta with grated cheese and chopped fresh herbs
- ✿ Fruit salad: Wash and peel (as necessary) a combination of the following fruits, chop them into bite-sized pieces, and toss them together in a bowl: watermelon, apple, orange, strawberries, blueberries, pineapple, grapes, mango, peach, kiwi fruit, passionfruit
- ✿ Power breakfast: vanilla yogurt, sliced banana, cereal or granola, drizzled honey
- ✿ Banana smoothie: blend banana, milk, Greek yogurt, honey, ice

CLASSIC RECIPES

Recipes that most people know and love are called "classics." Here are some simple and delicious examples to try out as you explore more things you can create in the kitchen. Many of these recipes use the oven or stove, or involve chopping ingredients with a knife, so make sure you get a grown-up to help you with these steps.

SHRIMP COCKTAIL

This dish is a true classic—simple and fresh!

Serves: 2

What you'll need:
- 1 tablespoon mayonnaise
- 1 tablespoon tomato sauce
- ½ teaspoon Worcestershire sauce
- 2 large iceberg lettuce leaves, shredded
- ½ avocado, sliced
- 1 lemon wedge
- 8 fresh shrimp cooked and peeled

What to do:
1. In a small bowl, mix together the mayonnaise, tomato sauce, and Worcestershire sauce until well combined. This is your sauce!

2. In two small serving bowls, fill the bottom with the chopped lettuce, then add the slices of avocado.

3. Put four shrimp into each bowl, then add a squeeze of fresh lemon. Top with the sauce and serve.

EASY LEMON ROAST CHICKEN

Everyone loves a good roast chicken. It's the ultimate comfort food. Serve with delicious roast potatoes.

What you'll need:

- 1 whole chicken
- 1 lemon, cut in half
- 2 sprigs fresh rosemary
- 2 tablespoons olive oil
- 6 sprigs fresh thyme, or 1 teaspoon dried thyme
- salt and pepper to season

What to do:

1. Pre-heat the oven to 350°F.

2. Rinse the chicken under cold running water, then pat it dry with a paper towel.

3. Place the chicken in a baking dish. Push both halves of the lemon and the sprigs of rosemary inside the cavity of the chicken, then tie the legs together with twine.

4. Rub the olive oil over the skin of the chicken, then season with thyme, salt, and pepper.

5. Roast for 20–25 minutes per pound (so, if your chicken is 3 lb, it will take a little over 60 minutes).

6. When the chicken is cooked, remove it from the oven, cover it with foil, and allow it to rest for 10 minutes before serving.

"APEELING" POTATOES

Who doesn't love potatoes? They might be everyone's favorite vegetable. Here's how to make two of the most popular potato dishes.

MASHED POTATOES

Serves: 4

What you'll need:

- 4–6 medium potatoes, peeled and quartered
- 2 tablespoons butter
- ¼ cup milk (or 2 tablespoons heavy cream and 2 tablespoons milk)
- salt and pepper to season

What to do:

1. Place the potatoes in a medium saucepan, cover them with cold water, and add a pinch of salt.

2. Bring water to boil over high heat, then reduce the heat to low and put the lid on. Allow the water to simmer for 15–20 minutes or until the potatoes are soft enough that you can easily poke a fork into them.

3. When the potatoes are cooked, transfer them to a colander to let the water drain out, then return them to the empty saucepan.

4. Mash the potatoes with a potato masher, then add the butter, milk, and seasoning to taste. Keep mashing until you've achieved a smooth texture.

ROAST POTATOES

What you'll need:
- 4 medium potatoes, quartered (peel them if you don't like the skin)
- 2–3 tablespoons olive oil
- salt and pepper to season
- 1–2 teaspoons dried thyme
- 2 crushed garlic cloves (optional – for garlicky potatoes)

Serves: 4

What to do:

1. Pre-heat the oven to 425°F and line a baking tray with parchment paper.

2. Place the potatoes in a medium saucepan, cover them with cold water, and add a pinch of salt. Bring the water to boil, then turn down the heat and allow the potatoes to simmer for about 10 minutes, before transferring them to a colander to let the water drain out. Be very careful because they'll be boiling hot.

3. Tip the potatoes onto the prepared baking tray. Drizzle them with olive oil and season them with salt, pepper, and thyme. Add the crushed garlic, if using.

4. Cook them in the oven for 30–40 minutes or until the potatoes are golden brown and crispy.

NO-BAKE LIME CHEESECAKE

The freshness of the lime adds an extra special zing to this old favorite.

What you'll need:

- 6 oz plain graham crackers
- ½ cup almond meal
- ¼ cup pure cream
- ⅓ cup butter, melted
- ¼ cup water
- 3 tablespoons gelatin powder
- 2½ cups cream cheese
- 1 cup light sour cream
- ¾ cup powdered sugar
- zest of two limes
- ½ cup lime juice
- whipped cream to serve (optional)

Serves: 8-10

What to do:

1. Line a large pie dish with parchment paper.

2. Break up the graham crackers and put them in a blender, then process until you have fine crumbs.

3. Transfer the graham cracker crumbs to a bowl. Add the almond meal, cream, and melted butter, and stir together. This will form the base of your cheesecake. Using your fingers, press the mixture into the dish until you've evenly covered the bottom all the way to the edges. Place in the fridge to chill.

4. Put the water in a small bowl, then add the gelatin powder one spoon at a time, whisking in each spoonful with a fork to avoid lumps.

5. In an electric mixer, beat the cream cheese until it's soft, then add the sour cream and sugar, mixing until smooth. Add the lime zest, lime juice, and dissolved gelatin, then keep mixing until everything is combined.

6. Take your base out of the fridge, pour in the cheesecake filling, and spread it so it covers the base evenly. Return the cheesecake to the fridge and allow it to set for at least 6 hours or overnight.

7. To serve, cut the cheesecake into slices and top each one with a dollop of whipped cream, if using.

FRENCH TOAST

Slices of bread that have started to go stale are perfect for French toast. Turn your old bread into this delicious weekend breakfast!

Serves: 2

What you'll need:

- 2 eggs
- 4 slices bread
- ½ cup milk
- topping such as strawberry jam, fresh berries, banana, syrup, or a sprinkle made by mixing 2 teaspoons white sugar and ½ teaspoon ground cinnamon to serve

What to do:

1. Take a wide bowl and break the eggs into it. Add the milk and whisk the eggs and milk together with a fork until it's well combined.

2. Pre-heat a non-stick frying pan to medium-high heat.

3. Dip the first slice of bread in the egg mixture for a few seconds until it's coated on both sides, then put it straight into the frying pan.

4. Cook for 2–3 minutes on either side, or until it's golden in color and no longer sticks to the pan.

5. Repeat for each slice of bread.

6. Serve with toppings.

STAINED-GLASS WINDOW GELATIN CAKE

Perfect for a birthday party, picnic, or special occasion. When you cut into it, each slice of this gelatin cake looks like a beautiful window in a cathedral with the light shining through.

Serves: 6

You'll need to start making this recipe 2 days ahead of when you want to eat it, as each stage takes time to set.

What you'll need:

- 3 packets sweetened gelatin mix (such as Jell-O), each a different color (have fun choosing)
- 3 tablespoons unflavored gelatin powder
- ½ cup cold water
- 1½ cups boiling water
- 1 14-oz can sweetened condensed milk
- ½ cup heavy whipping cream
- 1 teaspoon vanilla extract

What to do:

1. You'll need 3 separate square or rectangular dishes, one for each color. Make up the 3 gelatins according to the directions on the packet. Leave them in the fridge to set overnight.

2. Add the gelatin powder to the cold water one spoon at a time, whisking with a fork until the gelatin is fully dissolved. Add the boiling water and stir well. Then mix in the sweetened condensed milk, cream and vanilla extract. Let the mixture cool to room temperature.

3. Remove the 3 gelatins and chop them into uneven pieces.

4. Place all the different-colored gelatin pieces in a 2-litre bowl or dish.

5. Pour your cooled milk mixture carefully over your bowl of gelatin pieces, making sure they're spread through it evenly. Place the bowl in the fridge to set the mixture overnight.

6. To serve, immerse the bottom of the bowl in hot water for 2 minutes to loosen, then turn your colorful gelatin cake onto a nice plate, and cut it into slices.

ACTIVITY: DESIGN YOUR OWN MENU

Food is a wonderful way to bring everyone together.

Plan your own three-course menu, with appetizer, main course, and dessert. You can use the recipes in this book, or come up with some of your own! Once you've decided on your menu, you could then run a pop-up restaurant for family or friends. Think of what to call your restaurant, what your logo will look like, and how your menu would be designed. Then draw it up or type it up. When you open your restaurant for business, plan it so you can sit down with your customers and enjoy the meal with them!

WRITING IS A WONDERFUL PASTIME, and it can have all sorts of positive effects on your happiness and wellbeing. It can help you make a record of important times in your life, and make you think about things around you that you wouldn't ordinarily pay attention to. The possibilities are endless when it comes to writing—the only limit is your imagination!

Here are just some of the many different ways you can start writing—and who knows, one day you might even become a famous author! You can write by hand with a pen or pencil, or you can type on a computer—whatever feels best for you!

WRITE A STORY

Start with an idea. You might have a story you want to tell, or maybe you need to think about it for a bit. You can write a story about absolutely anything! Maybe there are books you enjoy reading, and you'd like to tell a similar story of your own. Your idea might also be about a particular character whose story you want to tell. Or perhaps your story is about something that really happened to you, or something you wish would happen.

The next step is to think about the characters in your story. Do you want your main character to be a child, an adult, an animal, or maybe even an alien? Also think about where your story will take place. This is called the "setting" and it might be your neighborhood, another country, in outer space, or in a magical land far, far away.

Then you'll need to work out what's going to happen to your main character. Will something go wrong that they need to fix? Will they go on a quest to find something? Are there other characters they'll meet along the way? Is there a villain? Or is it a love story? Is there something surprising that happens? How will your story work out in the end? Will it have a happy ending, or not? It's all up to you!

WRITE A PICTURE BOOK

In a book of blank paper, write a story for younger children. Alongside your story, you can draw illustrations too!

WRITE A MEMOIR

A memoir, or autobiography, is when someone writes their own life story. Why don't you take a shot at writing your life story? Try starting with a few different chapters that each show an important part of your life. These might be things such as:

* ❀ The very first thing you can remember
* ❀ Something surprising that happened to you
* ❀ A time when you learned something important
* ❀ Your favorite birthday
* ❀ A time when you made a mistake
* ❀ A time when you achieved something great
* ❀ Something you did that made you very nervous
* ❀ Your happiest memory
* ❀ Anything else that you think was a special moment

Remember to describe details such as what you were feeling at the time, how you feel about it now, and why this memory is important to you. You can also describe the people you were with, and where each memory happened.

KEEP A JOURNAL

Lots of people like to keep a journal. It's a lovely way to keep a record of memories and happy times that you might otherwise forget. It's also useful for better understanding your thoughts and feelings. Sometimes it can be difficult to express them out loud, but when you write about your feelings, as you spend time choosing the words, you might start to see things more clearly.

Each evening, write as much or as little as you want about what you experienced and thought that day. If you're too busy or tired one evening, you can simply list the day's activities or draw a picture of something you did. Write down some of the thoughts you had, or even have a conversation with your notebook! Pick a nice journal or buy a diary from a bookstore—it can be as plain or funky as you like! Make sure to put the date at the top of each entry.

There are other kinds of journals or diaries you can keep too. Some of these include:

- ✿ **A travel journal:** When you go on vacation, make a record of the things you see and do using a combination of writing, pictures, and souvenirs, such as tickets from flights, trains, or entry into museums, concerts, events, and other attractions.

- ✿ **A nature journal:** In this type of journal, you record observations about the things that fascinate you in the natural world. You might draw pictures and note the names of plant and animal species you spot, describe the sounds you hear, or jot down cool facts you learn. You can also paste into your journal interesting bits of nature, like leaves and feathers. If you go to the beach, draw some of the creatures you find living in the shells, but try not to disturb them too much! Also note that it's illegal to pick flowers or plants in a national park. Study the beauty of the natural world while being careful not to cause harm to any of its inhabitants!

WRITE A POEM

The first thing you probably think of when it comes to poetry is, "The cat sat on the mat with a rat." But there are lots of types of poem you could write. Your poetry could be about people you love, your favorite place, memories, things you don't understand, or a time you felt a strong emotion like happiness, sadness, love, fear, anger, surprise, or excitement. Or you could write about an animal, a time of day, a season, your favorite color, waking up in the morning, or a trip to the zoo. Poems can be happy or sad, funny or serious.

Rhyme is another thing to think about when writing poetry. In the following poem, the second and fourth lines end with a rhyming sound:

Roses are red
Violets are blue
You look like a donkey
And you smell like one too

This is known as a rhyming pattern. Have a go at writing your own "Roses are red, violets are blue" poem by adding two new lines to the end!

There are lots of other rhyming patterns. Then again, many poems don't rhyme at all. Research some poems in books and online to see which style you like the best. You could even start your own book of poetry! Why not challenge your family to a poetry competition one night? Everyone can write their own poem, and then you can take turns reading them out loud.

TIP

Try using a technique called "alliteration" in your poem. This is when different words that are close together start with the same sound. For example, "Peter Piper picked a peck of pickled peppers" or "She sells seashells by the sea shore."

Here are two different types of poems you could try.

LIMERICKS

Limericks are also called "nonsense poems" and they're lots of fun. They introduce a quirky character, they're funny, and they don't have to make any sense! Limericks have five lines, and you just need to make the first, second, and last lines rhyme together, while the third and fourth lines have a different rhyme. Here's an example:

There was an old man from the coast,
Who fancied a hot chicken roast.
His oven he overloaded,
Then the whole thing exploded,
So for dinner he decided on toast.

HAIKU

An ancient form of poetry from Japan, a haiku has three lines. The first and third lines are five syllables long, and the middle line has seven syllables. Haikus don't have to rhyme, but it's good if they evoke a particular mood or experience, especially to do with nature. This famous haiku was written by Matsuo Bashō, who was born around 1644.

Furu ike ya
kawazu tobikomu
mizu no oto

In English, this means:

The old pond.
A frog jumps in:
Plop!

FEATURED ORGANIZATION
iWRITE

Children's author Melissa Williams Murphy originally founded an organization called READ3Zero in Houston, Texas, to promote literacy among at-risk youth. When she realized on her school visits that students were interested in writing and publishing their own stories, she decided to shift the organization's focus, creating iWRITE in 2009. Since then, Melissa has developed camps and workshops that impart writing skills, confidence, and creativity while providing opportunities for kids to publish.

Each year, iWRITE hosts an annual writing and illustration contest where children submit their work to be published in an anthology titled *I Write Short Stories by Kids for Kids*. They can also send their stories to *iWRITER Magazine*—a quarterly publication that gives students real-life publishing experience.

Writing is such an important skill and tool of self-expression. It's also a great way to relieve stress, examine our thoughts and feelings, and share our ideas with others. Today, iWRITE reaches children well beyond Houston and across the globe through online learning.

HENRY PATTERSON
United Kingdom

By the time Henry Patterson was nine years old, he'd already tried out a few different business ideas. His first business was selling horse poop because his mom's horse made a lot of it! He started customizing his old toys and making toy boxes and selling them online. Then he decided to make his own collection of lollipops, including edible mud and worms, to sell to children.
Henry loves creating things!

When he was ten, Henry wrote a children's book called *The Adventures of Sherb and Pip* featuring Pip the adventure loving mouse, an owl called Sherb who's an inventor, and a badger called Brendan, who makes lemonade and plays the guitar. Henry and his mom brought these characters to life with their children's lifestyle store, Not Before Tea. Henry has appeared in lots of media in the United Kingdom as well as in other countries. He says a major challenge for him is school, because he can be appearing on popular TV program *The One Show* one day, and then in a math lesson the next.

In 2018, when he was fourteen, Henry published a book called *Young and Mighty*, a guide for kids to start their own businesses and turn their passions into more than just a hobby. For him, he says, success is waking up happy each day, excited to go to work and make a difference in both his life and the lives of other people. He encourages kids to figure out their own idea of success and go for it today!

ARTS AND CRAFTS

WHEN WE MAKE THINGS, we feel a sense of success and achievement. We also end up with something beautiful and unique! A craft is a skill that's usually decorative or that involves your hands. There are many types of crafts, including woodworking, pottery, knitting, sewing, quilting, beading and jewelry-making, toy-making, basket weaving, origami, papier-mâché, and flower arranging.

The beauty of crafts is that you end up with things that are one of a kind. This is the opposite of what we usually see in shopping malls and stores, which are packed with mass-produced items— things that are churned out quickly and cheaply and all look the same. With a craft, you know how much love, care, and time has gone into making something special. What's something you'd like to be able to create?

ACTIVITY: MAKE YOUR OWN PLAYING CARDS

Take some thick paper or cardstock and cut out 52 rectangles, all of the same size—add two more if you want to include jokers. Pick four suits: these can be the classics—hearts, diamonds, clubs, and spades—or you could come up with four suits of your own. Draw up your cards, and have fun dressing up your kings, queens, and jacks! Or you could pick a new theme for your playing cards, such as African animals or space!

PHOTOGRAPHY

It's easy to start being a photographer these days. You might have a professional digital single lens reflex (DSLR) camera at home, but if not, you can begin by using a smartphone. Here are some photography tips to help you take great photos.

- ❀ Good lighting is key to all good photos. If you're photographing a person, make sure they're facing the light source (in other words, the light isn't behind them). When taking photos outside, make sure the light isn't too dappled. When you're used to the basics, you can start exploring more artistic ideas and playing around with the contrast between dark and light.

- ❀ Don't always take your photos from the most obvious angle—try getting down low or up high with the camera. Keep moving around and experimenting with different angles.

- ❀ Sometimes, getting up really close to the subject of your photo can give you a fresh perspective.

- ❀ Think about composition: how the things in the photo are arranged, especially what's in the background. If something in the background is distracting or out of place, either move it, or adjust your composition.

- ❀ Don't cut off important parts of your subject, like the top of their head or their hands or feet. Either include all of their arms and hands, or just from the elbows upward.

ACTIVITY: A PHOTO JOURNAL

Go on a walk where the aim is to photograph things you find beautiful, interesting, or inspiring. Create a collage of photos that you can look at when you need a mood boost. You could create different albums with different themes. For example, one album could be pictures of things you see in the sky, such as clouds, the sun, moon, stars, rain, planes, balloons, birds, ducks, kites, or treetops. A happiness album could include pictures of things that make you happy, like people and pets. It's totally up to you!

SEWING

There are lots of simple and useful sewing skills you can learn, from how to sew on a button or fix a tear in your clothes, to bigger projects like making a quilt, pillow cases, or sewing your own clothes. If you have a craft store near you, it's bound to have all kinds of projects for you to try. Look on YouTube and you'll find lots of videos that show you the basics of sewing.

TIP

You don't have to buy all your sewing materials at once if you decide to make a quilt. Each time you visit the fabric store, just buy one more piece to add to your collection. You could also save your favorite childhood clothes and one day make a patchwork memory quilt from them.

LEARN NEW THINGS

YOU PROBABLY SPEND A LOT of time doing things you have to do for school. This can sometimes stop you from finding out what your other interests are, and what you're passionate about. Chances are, you find some subjects and classes at school more enjoyable than others, but what is it that you love doing most in the world? This can actually be quite a difficult thing to work out, and lots of adults are still trying to figure it out too!

The best way to discover what you're passionate about is to try new things, and learn new things. Explore!

Think about some of the activities you enjoy doing now, and some that you don't like as much. Now imagine waking up in the morning and preparing to do each of these things. Which ones make you want to leap out of bed and get started? Do any of them make you want to pull the blanket over your head and go back to sleep?

Here are some ideas for things you could learn, but the possibilities are endless. Think about something you'd like to be able to do one day—it could be as simple as learning how to crack an egg with one hand, or as complicated as building a computer—then plan a way to make it happen, now or in the future!

LEARN A NEW WORD ———————————————

Learning new things can actually be surprisingly easy, and it doesn't always have to involve learning something huge and difficult! It can be as simple as learning a new word each day, each week, or each month, and then seeing if you can use it when you're talking to people. To get you started, here are a few words and their meanings:

- ✿ Vocabulary—all the words or phrases in a language.
  E.g. I'm improving my vocabulary every day!

- ✿ Tomfoolery—silly or foolish behavior, like playing pranks.
  E.g. My tomfoolery makes everyone laugh.

- ✿ Rambunctious—noisy and energetic.
  E.g. My brother is very rambunctious. It's so annoying.

- ✿ Nostalgic—a longing for, or happy thoughts about, a time in the past.
  E.g. I feel nostalgic when I think about the house I grew up in.

- ✿ Vermillion—a deep and brilliant shade of red.
  E.g. Today, my favorite color is vermillion.

- ✿ Uncanny—strange in a mysterious way.
  E.g. I have an uncanny feeling that I'm being watched.

- ✿ Blabbermouth—someone who talks too much and gives away secrets.
  E.g. My neighbor is a real blabbermouth.
- ✿ Catastrophe—a disaster.
  E.g. I tried to bake a cake, and it was a catastrophe. There's icing on the ceiling.
- ✿ Dumbfounded—so astonished that you might be left speechless.
  E.g. He was dumbfounded by how bad the cake was.
- ✿ Finicky—fussy or picky.
  E.g. I'm very finicky about what I eat.
- ✿ Gibberish—speech or writing that makes no sense.
  E.g. Stop talking gibberish!
- ✿ Hunky-dory—all good.
  E.g. The sun was shining and everything was hunky-dory.
- ✿ Nincompoop—a foolish person.
  E.g. Her sister was being a real nincompoop.
- ✿ Zonked—tired.
  E.g. It had been a long day of learning new words, and he was totally zonked.
- ✿ Shenanigans—tricks or mischievous behavior.
  E.g. They were up to their usual shenanigans.

Keep a record of your new words in a notebook or in a document on your computer. You can even make your own dictionary of words! What's your favorite word?

LEARN ABOUT A NEW SPORT ——————

You might like some sports but not others, or maybe you don't like any sports at all! Why not learn the rules of a sport you don't know, and then watch it being played? Maybe after that you might like to play it too!

RUSSIAN
DOBROYE UTRO *OR* PRIVYET
POKA

GREEK
KALIMERA *OR* YIA SAS
GYIA SOU (TO ONE PERSON) *OR* YIA SAS (TO MULTIPLE PEOPLE)

ARABIC
AHLAN
MA'A AS-SALAAMA

JAPANESE
KONNICHIWA
SAYONARA

CANTONESE
NÉIH HÓU
JOI GIN

SPANISH
HOLA *OR* BUENOS DÍAS
ADIÓS

FRENCH
SALUT *OR* BONJOUR
AU REVOIR

— LEARN A LANGUAGE —

You might already know more than one language, but it's always fun to learn a new one, even if it's just a few words. There are lots of books to help you learn other languages, as well as classes you can take, free tutorials on YouTube, and language apps such as Duolingo. Start a journal with your favorite words and expressions in the language you want to learn!

MANDARIN
NI HAO
ZÀI JIÀN

KOREAN
ANNYEONG
ANNYEONGHI GASEYO

Here are some ways to say hello and goodbye in lots of different languages. There are plenty more that you can find in language books or online!

GERMAN
HALLO *OR* GUTEN TAG
AUF WIEDERSEHEN

TURKISH
SELAM *OR* MERHABA
GÜLE GÜLE (SAID TO THE PERSON LEAVING) *OR* HOŞÇA KAL (SAID TO THE PERSON STAYING)

ELVISH (QUENYA)
AIYA
NAMÁRIË

ITALIAN
BUONGIORNO
ARRIVEDERCI

ENGLISH
HELLO
GOODBYE

LEARN CODING

Learning how to code is a fun and useful activity that allows you to do things like make your own online games. Coding involves writing computer programs using programming languages, and it's a creative and satisfying skill. If you can code, you might one day make your own apps and video games! There are plenty of cool ways for you to learn to code online through playing games and doing puzzles. A good starting point is Scratch, a website offering a free programming language and illustrated tutorials that guide you to create your own interactive stories, games, and animations. Maybe have a look at code.org too. The site is famous for its hundreds of "hour of code" activities—hour-long tutorials based on Minecraft and characters from *Star Wars*, *Frozen*, and *Moana*.

ACTIVITY: WHAT ARE MY INTERESTS?

Here are some questions to think about that might help you discover what most interests you, and what you're passionate about. You can give more than one answer to each question. Do your best to think of things you genuinely enjoy—not things you feel you should answer with.

❀ If you had a two-week vacation starting tomorrow, what would you be most excited about doing?

❀ What's something you feel like you're good at?

❀ What's something you'd like to be good at but haven't done before?

❀ What are you saving up your money for?

❀ What have you done that made you feel the proudest you've ever been?

❀ What's something you dream of doing in the future that would make you feel proud to have achieved?

MUSIC

MAKING MUSIC IS SO MUCH FUN—it can take you into a world of your own and make you forget about everything else! Maybe you're already learning an instrument. If not, perhaps there are music classes at your school. Lots of people have an instrument at home but have never got around to learning how to play it. If that's your situation, perhaps you could look at free online lessons to start off with or, better still, get some one-on-one lessons.

If you don't own or have access to an instrument—guess what? We have the ability to make music with us all the time—using our voices. Sing along to your favorite songs, or find new songs that you'd like to learn.

Even if you don't play an instrument or want to learn one, there's a lot of enjoyment to be had from listening to music and exploring music from all different countries, cultures, and time periods. There's so much music available to us now on YouTube and apps like Spotify. Try listening to something you might not have thought you liked before. Here are some musical genres, or styles, you could explore:

- ✿ Classical
- ✿ Opera
- ✿ Jazz
- ✿ Blues
- ✿ Country
- ✿ Hip hop
- ✿ Rock
- ✿ Musical theatre
- ✿ Funk
- ✿ Rap
- ✿ Soul
- ✿ Electronic
- ✿ Folk

"MUSIC GIVES A SOUL TO THE UNIVERSE, WINGS TO THE MIND, FLIGHT TO THE IMAGINATION, AND LIFE TO EVERYTHING."

—PLATO, ANCIENT GREEK PHILOSOPHER

FEATURED ORGANIZATION
HARMONY PROJECT

Harmony Project is a Los Angeles–based organization that offers free, high-quality music instruction to students who wouldn't otherwise have the opportunity to learn an instrument.

Research has shown that children who engage with music tend to have greater focus and think critically and creatively. They're also likelier to perform well in school, attend college, and become successful adults. So, why doesn't everyone learn to play an instrument?

In some places around the United States, music isn't taught in schools. Private music lessons are also expensive and require resources like free time and transportation. To help more children access the benefits of music education, Harmony Project removes those barriers, providing free instruction, opportunities to perform, as well as academic and social support.

The program has been so successful that it has spread to other cities around the country. Today, Harmony Project serves 3,500 students in 16 different communities. Most of its graduates go on to higher education, and many continue to make music into adulthood.

AKIM CAMARA
Germany

Akim's father is from Nigeria and his mother is from Germany. When he was only two and a half years old, Akim began violin lessons. He still wore diapers and couldn't yet speak properly, but he could remember the names of all the instruments in an orchestra! And he seemed to have a natural instinct for remembering music.

At the age of three, Akim made his debut performance at a Christmas concert. Soon after, the famous violinist André Rieu saw Akim play and was so impressed that he invited Akim, his parents, and his grandmother to come to the Netherlands to André's studio. Two weeks later, wearing a tiny tuxedo and playing a miniature violin, Akim performed onstage with André supported by an orchestra in front of a crowd of 18,000 people. He received two standing ovations.

Akim's love of music is as strong as ever, but he's no longer interested in being in the public spotlight. Instead, he's chosen to continue studying music and practicing his violin in private. He can learn a piece of music after just one listen—amazing!

YOU MIGHT ALREADY BE A big reader, or maybe you haven't read a book for fun in a while. There's a book out there for everyone, so why not ask your parents if you can go to the library or your local bookstore to see if you can find the perfect book to take you away on a journey? There are lots of different kinds of books, from fantasy and adventure stories, to stories about real people, to books that teach you things. Try a few different types until you find something that you like. Reading a lot also helps you learn to be a better writer!

ACTIVITY: MAKE A LITTLE FREE LIBRARY FOR YOUR STREET

Little libraries, or neighborhood book exchanges, are small wooden boxes on streets where people can find and share books. Have you ever checked out any of these mini libraries near you? When you read a book you love, rather than have it gather dust on your bookshelf, you put it into a little library so others can enjoy it too. It's good to encourage friends and neighbors to do the same, so you can easily share your favorite stories. Why not help build one for your street? Go to littlefreelibrary.org/build and participate in this fantastic movement.

NEIGHBORHOOD BOOK EXCHANGE

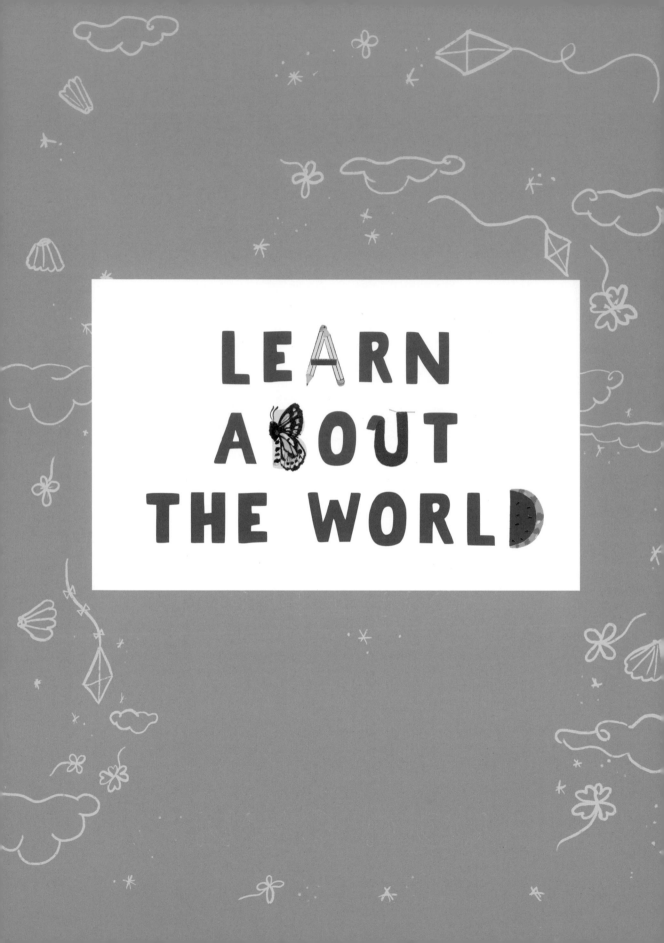

LEARN ABOUT THE WORLD

ARE YOU BURSTING WITH QUESTIONS all day long about why things are the way they are? There are loads of nifty ways to feed your curiosity about the world around you. Try some of the activities here, or do your own research into other STEM (science, technology, engineering, and math) projects to find out more about how the world works!

STEM ACTIVITY: MAKE A CLOUD

You might love cloud watching, but have you ever wondered how the clouds get up there? Clouds are made when water vapor condenses into droplets that attach to particles in the air. These water droplets then join together to create a cloud. There are billions of water droplets in an average-sized cloud! Here's how to make your own mini cloud in a jar.

What you'll need:

- a jar with a lid
- ⅓ cup hot water
- 4–6 ice cubes
- hairspray (to create your particles or pollution)

What to do:

1. Pour the hot water into the jar and give it a swirl so the inside of the jar gets warmed up.

2. Put the ice cubes in the lid of the jar, and then sit the lid upside down on top of the jar for about 30 seconds.

3. Lift up the lid, quickly spray a bit of hairspray into the jar, then put the lid back down.

4. A cloud will begin to form in your jar as the warm water turns into vapor. The vapor rises to the top of the jar where the air is cold due to the ice, which causes the vapor to condense. A cloud is made when the water vapor condenses on the particles of hairspray. In nature, these particles are usually things like dust, pollution, and pollen.

5. Once enough condensation has formed in the jar, remove the lid and your cloud will float out into the air.

STEM ACTIVITY: MAKE A BIRD'S NEST

Have you ever wondered how birds manage to build nests? They don't even have hands! Their beaks are actually very good tools for building and weaving! Using only what you can find outdoors—sticks, twigs, bark, leaves, thick grass, mud—see if you can build a nest as well as a bird can.

STEM ACTIVITY: MAKE A SUNDIAL

The ancient Egyptians were one of the first civilizations to divide the day into sections, using giant stone obelisks and noting where the shadows fell. Here's how to tell the time by the sun using the same technique.

What you'll need:
- Permanent marker or paints
- 9 rocks
- 1 stick

What to do:

1. Use a permanent marker or paints to number your rocks with each hour from 9 a.m. to 5 p.m.

2. Find a spot that stays in full sun all day and push the stick into the ground so it's standing up straight. Make sure it's casting a full shadow. When it's exactly 9 a.m., place your 9 a.m. rock where the shadow is being cast.

3. Every hour, place the rock with the number for the next hour where the shadow is being cast by the stick.

4. When it gets to 5 p.m., put down your last rock. Tomorrow, you'll have your very own sundial to tell the time.

STEM ACTIVITY: EXPERIMENT WITH BONES

This super-cool experiment lets you see the real-life effect that calcium and collagen have on our bones, and why we need them.

What you'll need:

- 3 chicken bones, cleaned and with as much meat removed as possible
- a small saucepan and access to water
- tongs
- 3 glasses or repurposed glass jars, big enough to hold one chicken bone each
- enough white vinegar to fill one jar
- enough bleach to fill the second jar
- enough water to fill the third jar
- paper towel

Note:
Find an adult to supervise. This activity uses bleach, which can stain your clothes and harm your skin. Take care not to spill or touch the bleach. Also be careful not to breathe in the fumes as they can hurt your eyes, nose, and lungs.

What to do:

1. Put the 3 bones in the saucepan and cover them with water. Bring the water to a slow boil, and boil the bones for 30 minutes. Remove the bones from the water, using the tongs, and set them aside to allow them to cool. Once they're cool, see if you can bend the bones. They're pretty hard, aren't they?

2. Place one bone in each of the three jars. Then cover one bone with vinegar, one with bleach, and one with water.

3. Leave the bones to soak in their liquids for 24 hours.

4. Use tongs to remove each bone from its container, rinse the bones off with water, and place them on a paper towel. Now, try to bend the bones again. Which one is the most bendy? What's changed?

5. You can continue soaking each bone in their liquids for another 2 days, then check back in again.

Calcium is a mineral that makes our bones stiff, so we can stand up, walk around, and lift things. But our bones also need to be a little bit flexible so they don't break! This is where a protein called collagen comes in. In your experiment, the acid in the vinegar dissolves the calcium but leaves the collagen, so the bones become super bendy and flexible. The bleach breaks apart the collagen proteins but leaves the calcium, so the bones become brittle and hard. Nothing noticeable happens to the bone soaked in water—this is your control in the experiment: you can compare this bone to the others and see how they've changed. So, remember to eat lots of healthy foods full of calcium and protein!

GET
PRACTICAL

ALONG WITH LEARNING NEW CREATIVE things, there are lots of practical things you could learn, such as cooking, ironing, doing the laundry, woodworking, and pottery. You can find videos on a whole range of topics on TED-Ed at ed.ted.com.

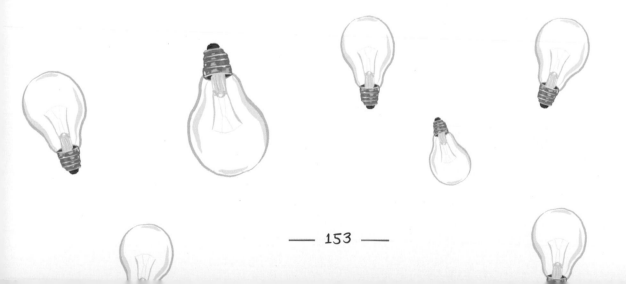

HOME
AND
LIFESTYLE

AN IMPORTANT PART OF FEELING optimistic and good about life is making sure our surroundings are cozy and safe. We all need to have a space where we can feel comfortable and relaxed. This involves having delicious food to nourish us, decorating our living spaces to make sure they're homey and we feel happy there, and taking time to tend to our plants and gardens. This chapter explores ways you can start living on the bright side at home.

BRAIN FOOD

EATING A BALANCED DIET IS very important for being more optimistic. As well as satisfying our hungry tummies, regular meals and good food give us energy and make us strong and healthy. Preparing meals and thinking up new recipes is also lots of fun.

On the other hand, there's nothing that makes us grumpier than being hungry! When we don't eat well—for example, if we eat a whole bag of candy by mistake when we only intended to eat one or two pieces—it can put us in a bad mood.

The recipes on the following pages are for healthy meals (and treats!) to help keep you feeling fine and focused throughout the day, and stop you from becoming a bad-mood bear.

> **"ONE CANNOT THINK WELL, LOVE WELL, SLEEP WELL, IF ONE HAS NOT DINED WELL."**
> —VIRGINIA WOOLF, ENGLISH WRITER

BREAKFAST BAKED EGG CUPS

Try this quick and easy recipe to kickstart your morning. Eggs are packed with protein, vitamins, iron, choline, and omega 3, all of which are very important for brain development. Plus, they keep you feeling full for longer so you don't get hangry later on! Add spinach for vitamin B6, which is essential for our mental health.

Serves: 1

What you'll need:

- 2 slices of ham or strips of bacon
- 2 eggs
- 2 teaspoons fresh parsley and/or chives, roughly chopped
- ¼ cup baby spinach (optional)
- grated cheese to sprinkle on top
- salt and pepper

What to do:

1. Pre-heat the oven to 400°F.

2. Grease two cups of a muffin tray or two small ramekins with butter or oil, then lay the slices of ham in the base. If you're using bacon, cut the strips in half diagonally.

3. Crack one egg into each of the cups.

4. Top with chopped herbs, baby spinach (if using), and grated cheese, then season with salt and pepper.

5. Bake in the oven for 10–12 minutes. Allow to cool slightly, then ask a grown-up to help you remove the egg cups using a pair of tongs.

LUNCH
RICE PAPER ROLLS

Serves: 2

There's nothing fresher and more vibrant than rice paper rolls, which are so good for a summertime lunch, served with a tasty peanut satay sauce. Sweet chilli sauce also works well. If you don't like shrimp, you can use shredded chicken instead. Shrimp and chicken are both excellent sources of vitamin B3 (niacin), which has been shown to improve memory.

What you'll need:

FOR THE WRAPS

- vermicelli noodles, cooked according to the directions on the packet
- 6 rice paper wraps
- 8 shrimp, cooked and peeled
- 12 mint leaves
- 1 carrot, peeled and chopped into matchsticks
- 1 small cucumber, cut into matchsticks
- 1 avocado, cut in half, peeled and sliced
- ⅓ cup roughly chopped cilantro

FOR THE SATAY DIPPING SAUCE

- ½ cup water
- 2 tablespoons unsalted peanut butter
- 1 tablespoon soy sauce
- the juice of half a lime
- 1 teaspoon honey

What to do:

1. First make the dipping sauce. Place the water, peanut butter, soy sauce, lime juice, and honey in a small saucepan. Stir with a whisk over medium heat until heated through and thickened. Remove from the heat and allow to cool to room temperature.

2. Now make the rice paper rolls. Dip the first rice paper wrap in a bowl of warm water for a few seconds, then lay it carefully on a plate.

3. In the centre of your wrap, place 3 shrimp next to each other, then top with 2 mint leaves, a few sticks of carrot and cucumber, a layer of avocado, a sprinkling of cilantro, then some vermicelli noodles.

4. Fold the bottom half of your rice paper wrap up and over the stack, then fold the sides over. Tightly roll up your wrap.

5. Repeat with the remaining 5 wraps until you have 6 rolls. Serve with the satay dipping sauce or sweet chilli sauce.

DINNER
HONEY SOY SALMON AND BROCCOLI

Serves: 2

When it comes to brain food, you can't forget oily fish, such as salmon, mackerel, and sardines. Salmon is high in omega-3 fatty acids, which are extremely important for our brain health. In fact, our brains are 60 percent fat! Salmon is also a good source of your B vitamins. And we all know how healthy broccoli is, but did you know that it can also help with your mental health? Broccoli is packed with glutamine, vitamin B5, and folic acid, which are all beneficial for our wellbeing.

What you'll need:

- 2 cloves garlic, minced
- 1 teaspoon minced ginger
- ⅓ cup soy sauce
- 2 tablespoons honey
- 2 pieces salmon, skin on
- 1 broccoli head
- lemon wedges to serve
- boiled or steamed rice to serve (optional)

What to do:

1. Pre-heat the oven to 400°F.

2. Line a baking tray with parchment paper.

3. In a bowl, combine the garlic, ginger, soy sauce, and honey.

4. Coat the salmon pieces with the honey and soy sauce mixture, then place the salmon on the baking tray, skin side down, and bake for 15–20 minutes.

5. Meanwhile, wash your broccoli and chop it up into florets.

6. Bring a saucepan of water to boil. Add the broccoli florets and cook, uncovered, for about 3–4 minutes. Drain through a colander.

7. Remove the salmon from the oven. Arrange on plates—on a bed of rice if you want a heartier meal—and serve with the broccoli, wedge of lemon, and any sauce from around the salmon.

DESSERT
CHOCOLATE AND BANANA POPS

Bananas are loaded with nutrients, such as potassium, magnesium, iron, calcium, folate, and vitamin B6. They're also rich in an amino acid called tryptophan, which is great for lifting your mood and helping you sleep well. So, not only are bananas terrific for powering up your brain, they're also delicious, especially when covered in chocolate, which happens to be a fantastic source of magnesium!

Serves: 6

What you'll need:

- 6 repurposed popsicle sticks (collect these after finishing your frozen treat—try to remember not to chew them up!)
- ½ cup milk, dark, or white chocolate
- 3 bananas, peeled and cut in half
- ½ cup crushed or roughly chopped peanuts or sprinkles

What to do:

1. Line a tray with parchment paper.

2. Break the chocolate into small pieces and put it in a glass microwave-proof bowl. Microwave at 20-second intervals, stirring between each interval, until the chocolate is almost melted. Stir until the last of the chocolate melts.

3. Insert the popsicle sticks in the bottom of each of your 6 banana pieces. One at a time, dip each banana into the chocolate, using a spoon to make sure they're fully coated.

4. Sprinkle each banana with the peanuts, then place on the tray.

5. Refrigerate for 60 minutes or until the chocolate is firm.

DRINKS

For these healthy and refreshing juice ideas, all you have to do is chop up the ingredients, pop them in a blender, and get mixing! It's ready to drink right away, but you can strain the juice—into your glass if you don't like the pulpy bits. If you need more liquid, add half a cup of coconut water.

SUPER STRENGTH

- 4 strawberries
- 1 apple
- 4 chunks of pineapple
- handful of spinach
- 4–6 ice cubes

BERRY DELICIOUS

- 2 apples
- handful of blueberries
- handful of raspberries
- 6 strawberries
- 4–6 ice cubes

COOL AS A CUCUMBER

- 1 cup grapes
- 2 oranges
- handful of blueberries
- 1 small cucumber
- 4–6 ice cubes

WATERMELON WONDER

- 2 cups fresh watermelon (preferably chilled)
- 4 strawberries
- 1 apple
- 4 mint leaves
- 8 ice cubes

TIP

For a healthy snack, choose nuts and seeds. They'll boost your omega 3, magnesium, and protein.

DECORATE YOUR SPACE

CLEANING AND ORGANIZING YOUR BEDROOM might not sound like your idea of a good time, but making a nice space that's uniquely yours can actually be a lot of fun. Tidying up a space is also a good way to tidy up your mind. When our surroundings are messy and cluttered, our thoughts can become messy too. There's evidence that a cluttered bedroom with clothing everywhere and stacks of books and papers on every surface can make it difficult to fall asleep at night. But a neat and ordered space is peaceful and has a calming effect. And you might feel proud when you have friends over and you can bring them into your room!

Here are some tips for ways you can spruce up your room and calm your mind at the same time.

DIY BEDROOM IDEAS

- ❀ Pick a theme for your room. It could be an interesting color combination, a favorite animal, or a setting like the beach, the forest, or under the sea. Draw and cut out pictures and put them on the walls.
- ❀ Create your own posters and paintings.
- ❀ Add a nice rug to the floor.
- ❀ Reorganize your bookshelf so your books are grouped together by color—it will look like a rainbow!
- ❀ Clear your surfaces. Organize your papers into folders and recycle any you don't need.
- ❀ Place a small laundry basket in the corner. Instead of throwing your dirty clothing on the floor or hanging it over the back of a chair, you can toss it in the basket.
- ❀ Ask your parents to take you to a thrift store to hunt for new decorations.
- ❀ Make your own desk storage—use an old cardboard box and decorate it by painting it or sticking wrapping paper around the outside. Create pencil holders out of old jars.

- ✿ Make sure all the things you own have a place where you can put them away.

- ✿ Redecorate an old picture frame using paints. Try these patterns: dots, stripes, stars, zebra pattern, or a watermelon pattern.

- ✿ For a space theme, draw all the planets and stick them to your ceiling. Or you can print out pictures of them and cut them out.

- ✿ Make lavender wreaths or dried lavender bags—having lavender in your bedroom can help you sleep.

- ✿ Bring the outdoors inside: pick a bunch of flowers and arrange them in a vase, or collect pretty leaves and stones and put them in jars.

- ✿ Put plants in your room and around the house—plants provide oxygen, clean the air, and look pretty. Remember to water them once a week!

DID YOU KNOW?

Colors and emotions are connected, and different colors can affect our mood. Warm colors, such as red, orange, and yellow, can make people feel more energetic, but also feel more passion and anger. Warm colors can even make you feel hungry! Cool colors, with undertones of blue, green, and purple, are the most calming. People also often find that bright and light colors are more peaceful than deep and intense colors. But everyone's responses to color are different, and they change depending on your personal experience and culture. Explore how different colors make you feel, then decorate your room with the colors that make you calmest, happiest, and coziest.

HOW TO DRY LAVENDER

If you or someone you know has lots of lavender growing, grab some! It's very easy to dry it out. Lavender looks and smells beautiful when it's hanging in bunches while it's drying. Once it's dry you can make little lavender bags to keep in your clothes drawer to freshen up those stinky socks!

What you'll need:

- a large bunch of lavender flowers with plenty of stalk left on
- string
- scissors

What to do:

1. Divide the lavender into bundles and tie each bundle with string.
2. Hang the bundles upside down from a hook on your wall or near a window that gets plenty of sun.
3. In about 2–4 weeks, your lavender will be dry.
4. You can chop up your dried lavender, wrap it in fabric and tie the top with ribbon to make a lavender bag for your clothes drawer.

"THERE IS NOTHING LIKE STAYING AT HOME FOR REAL COMFORT."

—JANE AUSTEN, ENGLISH NOVELIST

ACTIVITY: MAKE A COMFY CUBBY

If you don't want to decorate your whole bedroom,
make a cubby full of relaxing things instead. This will be a
place you can go to relax, read a book, draw a picture,
have a nap, daydream, and think about the little
things in life that make you happy.

What to put in your cubby:

- ✿ Lots of cushions
- ✿ Blankets
- ✿ Your favorite toys
- ✿ A stack of your favorite books or comics
- ✿ A lamp
- ✿ Games to play
- ✿ Activity or coloring books
- ✿ Snacks

HYGGE (PRONOUNCED HOO-GUH) is a Danish word that means something like "coziness." It's the feeling you get when it's cold outside, but you're warm and snug and drinking hot chocolate by the fire. It's about enjoying the good and simple things in life, like sitting around the table with family, hugging the people you love, feeling safe at home, or enjoying a pastry. It's about remembering to relax and find joy in small moments when things feel overwhelming.

People who live this way are often happier because they take the time to concentrate on these warm and peaceful feelings whenever they can.

Here are some ways you can start. Try putting aside one day a week to spend with your family doing some of these things. These ideas work best on cold winter days, but you can find things to do in the summer too, like having an icy cold drink when it's hot outside, or feeling the water from the pool, ocean, or even a cool bath run over your skin.

- ✿ Ask your parents if you can light candles at nighttime (remember never to leave a burning candle unattended). Or you could look into getting battery-powered candles. Candlelight makes everything more relaxing and creates a calm atmosphere.
- ✿ Make the lights dim, or don't turn on too many lights. Just a lamp will do.
- ✿ Have a warm drink on a cold day. Put marshmallows in your hot chocolate!
- ✿ Organize a board game to play with your family one night. You might even like to set up a special place to play, with blankets, pillows, and snacks.
- ✿ Do a jigsaw puzzle.
- ✿ Wear socks!
- ✿ Wear your softest, comfiest clothes.
- ✿ When it's raining outside, get under a blanket and watch a movie with your family.
- ✿ Eat soup.

✿ Read a book together—take turns being the person to read to the rest of your family.

✿ Turn down the lights, prepare some warm milk and cookies, and listen to an audiobook.

✿ Relax in an armchair.

✿ Have a bubble bath.

✿ If you have a phone or tablet, turn it off in the evening.

✿ Bake something comforting with your family, like cookies, a cake, or muffins.

CHEERING HOT CHOCOLATE

A mug of hot chocolate cheers everyone up, even on the gloomiest of winter days—and sometimes in the summer too! When you've been playing outside in the cold, there's nothing better than coming indoors to warm up your hands with a hot drink.

What you'll need:

- 4 cups milk of your choice
- 4 tablespoons unsweetened cocoa powder
- 4 tablespoons granulated sugar (or maple syrup)
- 1 teaspoon vanilla extract
- marshmallows and whipped cream to serve (optional)

What to do:

1. In a saucepan, warm the milk.

2. Add the cocoa powder and sugar and whisk well until it's smooth and hot, but not boiling.

3. Remove from the heat and stir in the vanilla extract.

4. Pour into mugs and top with marshmallows and whipped cream, if using. Delicious!

Makes: 4 cups

HOMEMADE CHAI LATTE

This gently spiced drink is sure to make you feel cozy inside and out. You can almost imagine the snow falling outside and the fireplace roaring.

What you'll need:

- 2 cups water
- 2 tablespoons black tea leaves (or about 4 teabags)
- 2 tablespoons brown sugar (or maple syrup)
- 1 cinnamon stick
- 1 star anise, gently crushed
- 6 cardamom pods, gently crushed
- 4 cloves
- 1 teaspoon ground nutmeg
- ¼ teaspoon black peppercorns
- ½ teaspoon ground ginger
- 2 teaspoons vanilla extract
- 2 cups milk (you can use cow's milk or dairy-free alternatives like soy, nut, coconut, and oat milks)
- whipped cream to serve (optional)

Makes: 4 cups

What to do:

1. In a saucepan, add the water, tea leaves, brown sugar, cinnamon stick, star anise, cardamom pods, cloves, nutmeg, peppercorns, ginger, and vanilla extract, and stir to combine.

2. Place the saucepan on the stove, bring to a simmer, and allow to simmer for about 10 minutes, stirring occasionally.

3. Using a mesh strainer, strain your chai mixture and divide it evenly between four mugs. If you don't use all of it, the chai mixture can be kept in a repurposed jar in the fridge.

4. In the microwave or on the stove, heat up your milk. Once the milk is hot, not boiling, put it in an airtight jar and shake it until frothy—wrap the jar in a tea towel as it will be hot! You can also use an electric milk frother if you have one.

5. Add the milk to your tea. Top with whipped cream, if using, and enjoy!

SOOTHING SMELLS

SMELL IS ONE OF THE most influential senses when it comes to mood. Our sense of smell is directly linked to the emotional center of our brains, and is strongly connected to our memories and past experiences. You might notice this when the first warm spring breeze blows and you suddenly feel nostalgic or strangely wistful. Because of this powerful connection to our mood, different scents can do amazing things for our minds and bodies, from relieving headaches to helping us sleep or giving us more energy. Having pleasant smells in your bedroom at night can even help reduce nightmares!

Once you're aware of which smells make you happy, there are lots of ways you can bring them into your home. This could be from essential oils, candles, fresh flowers and herbs, pine cones, or baking bread.

Here are some different scents and the positive effects they can have:

- ✿ **Lavender:** for relaxation and sleep
- ✿ **Peppermint:** for headaches and improving concentration
- ✿ **Vanilla:** for joy and happiness, coziness and safety
- ✿ **Citrus:** for energy
- ✿ **Jasmine:** for confidence and optimism

As you go about your day, take a moment to pause when you notice pleasant scents around you. Smell flowers when you get the chance! Smell the seasons: the warm spring air in the petals of roses; the salt of the sea in summer, backyard barbecues, and the heat rising from the tar on the road; in autumn, smell the drying leaves and the earthiness as they turn to dirt, or the cinnamon-sweet smell of apple pie and fresh pastries; and in winter, smell the rain and woodfire smoke in the crisp air. How do these smells make you feel? Sometimes they might make you nostalgic, or even a little melancholy, and at other times they might fill you with joy or peace.

WHAT IS IT?

Petrichor—the fresh, earthy smell that often comes with the first rain after the weather has been warm and dry and the ground is hot. Interestingly, the word petrichor was actually made up by two researchers in the 1960s. The smell is partly caused by fragrant chemical compounds, including oils made by plants, but it's mainly caused by microorganisms called actinobacteria. When these bacteria decompose organic matter into nutrients for plants and other organisms, they also create an organic compound called geosmin—which adds to the petrichor smell. Then, when the ground gets humid and wet before it rains, as raindrops begin to hit the dry earth, they gather the geosmin and other petrichor compounds and send tiny particles of spray called aerosols into the air, which get carried by the wind and into our noses!

ACTIVITY: HOMEMADE DIFFUSER

Store-bought diffusers often contain artificial fragrances, which can smell too strong and give some people a headache. This homemade, all-natural diffuser will make any room smell amazing, it looks stylish, is fun to make, and its cost is minimal. Plus, you can personalize your bottle to make a great gift!

What you'll need:

❀ a small vase or bottle—like a cute repurposed glass bottle from the kitchen. It works best if you can find one with a narrow neck, but a jar will work too, although the liquid will evaporate more quickly

❀ 30–40 drops of an essential oil, such as lavender, grapefruit, chamomile, rose, geranium, or ylang ylang—these are just a few of the many essential oils you can choose from, or you could make your own combination of oils

❀ ½ cup unscented (or lightly scented) oil, such as grapeseed, safflower, or canola

❀ 6 bamboo skewers with the pointy tips cut off

What to do:

1. Add the essential oil and unscented oil to your bottle or jar and mix well.

2. Stick the bamboo skewers in your bottle. It may take a few hours for the scent to travel up the skewer. Every few days, turn the skewers around, placing the other end in the oil to give you a stronger scent.

PLANTING AND GARDENING TIPS AND TRICKS

GARDENING AND GROWING PLANTS HAVE been proven to boost your mood. Practicing mindfulness and nurturing your plants lowers stress, and keeps you connected to the outdoors and living things. Plants are also wonderful companions, and it can be a joyful experience to be responsible for them, look after them, and watch them grow. And in return, they provide us with beauty and fresh air. Gardening has even been prescribed to some patients with anxiety and depression.

What's your favorite plant? Would you rather grow things you can eat, such as herbs, fruits, and vegetables; do you prefer things that are pretty and smell nice, like flowers; or maybe you prefer unusual or exotic plants with unique leaves and strange-looking flowers? Whatever plants strike your fancy, you can start growing them, whether it's in an outdoor garden, on your balcony, on your windowsill, or even in water!

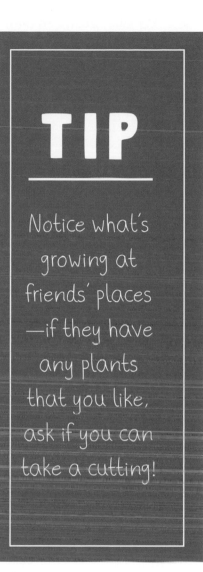

TIP

Notice what's growing at friends' places —if they have any plants that you like, ask if you can take a cutting!

PLANTS

These are some popular plants and flowers that can be rooted in water. For added decoration, you can fill the bottom of your glass or jar with pebbles and fancy stones.

- ✿ Lavender
- ✿ Philodendron
- ✿ Pothos

- ✿ African violets
- ✿ Inch plant
- ✿ Begonia
- ✿ Spider plants
- ✿ Polka dot plant
- ✿ Impatiens
- ✿ Money tree (or jade plant)
- ✿ Most succulents (just make sure you wait for the cut stem to dry up before placing it in water)

MORE PLANTS FOR LESS MONEY—PLANT CLONES

Most people buy their plants from a nursery or garden center, but have you ever taken a piece from a plant and got it to grow? This works for lots of plant species. These pieces, called cuttings, grow new roots in water very easily, giving you a clone of your original plant. So cool! All you need is a simple drinking glass, vase, or repurposed jar that's big enough to hold your plant babies.

What to do:

1. Choose a healthy mother plant that's large enough that you can take one or two cuttings without harming it.
2. Look for green stems at the tips of the mother plant to take as cuttings (green stems tend to grow new roots more readily than the woody brown stems)—a length of stem anywhere from about 2–6 in works well, depending on the size of the plant. Find a stem that has a node (the area where there's a leaf attached)—this is the place where new roots will grow. (Note that not all plants have nodes or will grow like this.)
3. Using scissors, cut just below this node.
4. Starting at the bottom of the stem, remove all but a few leaves at the top. Leaves cause the plant to use up energy, and you want to free up energy for making new roots. However, the cutting still needs some

leaves so it can continue photosynthesis to get its food while it's not getting any from the roots.

5. Find a glass or jar that's the right size for the leaves to stick out the top, then fill it with enough water to cover the stem. Place it in a well-lit spot that gets at least 6 hours of sunlight each day—a windowsill is perfect. If the water level gets too low, just top it up. Change the water every couple of days to stop the growth of mold or algae.

6. Keep your plants in the water until they've developed a whole root system, with roots at least 2–3 in long. Roots will usually develop over about 2–6 weeks. Eventually the plants will need more nutrients than the water can provide. If you're rooting your plants at the beginning of spring, you can transfer your new plants into a pot filled with potting mix. Note that not all plants will survive being transplanted into soil, so it's good to have a few cuttings. Remember to keep the soil around your newly potted plant moist but not soggy, as the plant is used to being in water.

If you end up with too many plants, you can put them in pretty pots and give them away as gifts!

DID YOU KNOW?

The plant that you take your cuttings from is called the mother plant.

PERENNIALS VS ANNUALS

Perennial plants live for several seasons or years. The top part of a perennial dies back in winter, but when spring comes around, new growth appears. The flowers on perennials usually bloom only for 2–6 weeks. Annual plants flower then die off in just one season, but they usually bloom all season long. A mix of both perennials and annuals in your garden makes sure you get plenty of variety. The different blooming times of the plants creates a habitat for pollinators like bees, butterflies, and other insects.

HERBS

At the end of summer when the weather starts to cool down, all of our fresh-grown herbs start to die off. But did you know you can keep growing some of these herbs in water until spring comes around again? Take cuttings of perennial herbs—even herbs bought from the supermarket can work—and place them in jars full of ordinary tap water. Arrange these on a sunny windowsill. Not only does this spruce up the room, it means you'll have a supply of fresh herbs through the winter! Change the water when it gets murky.

Here are some herbs that are good for growing in water.

- ❀ Basil
- ❀ Rosemary
- ❀ Mint
- ❀ Sage
- ❀ Lemon verbena
- ❀ Oregano

MO BRIDGES
United States of America

Moziah Bridges grew up in Memphis, Tennessee. When Mo was little, he always chose to wear a suit and tie. He really liked to dress up and look smart, and he absolutely loved bow ties! The trouble was that he couldn't find any bow ties that really "spoke" to him and that fit his style and personality. So, he started making his own. His grandmother taught him to sew his first bow tie!

In 2011, when Mo was nine years old, he and his mom started a business called Mo's Bows in his grandmother's kitchen. They started selling his bow-tie creations on Etsy and then through some boutique stores. Now, Mo is the President and Creative Director of Mo's Bows, which has become an internationally recognized brand. He says his mom is still the one who holds Mo's Bows together.

Along with bow ties, Mo's Bows make neckties and pocket squares. They've also started a foundation that aims to help other kids follow their passions and become leaders and inventors. Mo's advice for people who want to start their own business is to figure out what they like, then figure out how to make money from it.

Mo has begun studying fashion design in college. As he said on Steve Harvey's talk show, "Bow ties make you look good, and they make you feel good!" Mo certainly looks sharp!

GROWING VEGETABLES IN WATER

VEGETABLES SUCH AS SPRING ONIONS, leeks, celery, fennel, sweet potatoes, and lettuces can also sprout in water. This is a great way to use these vegetable scraps that you'd otherwise throw away, which means you're also reducing your food waste. Win–win!

VEGETABLES WITH A BULB

Because we only use the tops of veggies like spring onions, leeks, and fennel, we tend to discard the base without a second thought. Instead of throwing these away, you can actually regrow them! Put the stumps in a glass of water, root-end down, place them on a sunny windowsill, and they'll start to regrow their tops in just a few days. Change the water every day or two. You can either wait until they're big enough then cut the tops off to cook—and the process will start all over again—or you can plant them out in a pot of soil to finish growing.

ROOT VEGETABLES

With carrots and other root veggies that have their leaves attached, such as beetroots, you can't regrow the actual root in water, but you can sprout the leaves to add to salads!

Cut the tops off your carrots and beets and place them cut side down in a shallow dish of water with the leaves sticking out. Put the dish on a sunny windowsill and change the water each day. The tops will sprout shoots that you can eat! You can also plant the tops in soil once leaves have sprouted.

VEGETABLES WITH A HEAD

Similar to the bulb veggies, for vegetables with a head, such as lettuce, cabbage, celery, and bok choy, you can just cut off the base and place them cut side facing up in a shallow dish of water. Leafy scraps will grow on a sunny windowsill, or you can transplant them into soil once they have new roots and growth.

DID YOU KNOW?

You can use carrot leaves as you would an herb. The fine green leaves—avoid the fibrous stems— are full of vitamins and minerals and have a peppery, bitter flavor, halfway between carrots and parsley. Add them to a homemade pesto, toss them in a salad, or use them as a garnish for soup or roast vegetables.

SWEET POTATOES

"Slips" are green vines that grow when the sweet potato sprouts. These can be removed and planted in the ground to make a new sweet potato plant. You can buy sweet potato slips from plant nurseries, but you can also grow your own!

Find the pointed end of your sweet potato. Sit the sweet potato in a jar of water, pointed end first. You'll want to keep the top one-third of your potato completely out of the water. To do this, insert toothpicks into the sides so that they stick out over the top of the jar and hold the weight of the sweet potato. In a few weeks, a vine should begin to sprout. Once your sweet potato has lots of sprouts, carefully twist them off, separate them, and then root them in water. Once they have enough roots, these new slips will be ready to plant! Sweet potatoes need good drainage and warm conditions, so plant your slips in the spring time.

TIP

Some sweet potatoes that you buy in stores are treated to stop them from sprouting. Try to buy organic sweet potatoes as they are less likely to be treated.

EASY-CARE PLANTS

NOT ALL OF US CAN remember to take care of our plants and water them often. If that's you, don't worry. It's possible to have nice plants around you—and enjoy growing them—if you choose the right plants for you. Here's a list of houseplants that you don't need to worry about too much, but still look awesome.

- ❀ **Aloe vera**—very popular because as well as needing hardly any attention, the gel in its leaves can be used to soothe sunburn. Aloe doesn't mind dry soil, but it does prefer to be in a well-lit spot that's out of direct sunlight.

- ❀ **Snake plant**—can go for weeks without water and will survive in both low and bright light.

- ❀ **Ponytail palm**—a very cute palm plant that, as its name suggests, looks like it has a swishy ponytail. Keep it in a smaller pot to limit its growth.

- ❀ **Sago palm**—this plant does better when you forget to water it! Gives any room a tropical vibe.

- ❀ **Panda plant**—has the softest, furriest leaves that feel a bit like felt. Needs lots of bright light, but likes dry soil between waterings.

- ❀ **Living stones**—super cool succulents that look like rocks! They have big roots so will need a large pot, but they don't need any water in winter, just a little drink every few weeks in spring and summer.

- ❀ **Golden barrel cactus**—with spiky yellow spines, this striking cactus grows well indoors with plenty of bright light.

- ❀ **Bunny ear cactus**—originating in Mexico, this cactus loves desert-like conditions with plenty of sun. It's furry and has ears like a rabbit!

FASHION

PEOPLE USE CLOTHING AND FASHION in all different ways. Sometimes they want to be noticed and stand out from the crowd, and sometimes they want to fit in. And sometimes they don't care what anyone else thinks and they just wear whatever they want! All of these things are fine as long as you feel good about being you.

One of the best ways we can express ourselves is to wear things that feel truly "us"! Go through your wardrobe and pick out the things that make you feel most comfortable and confident. Go thrifting and see if you can find more things that really feel like you. While you're there, try out styles you might not have thought of wearing before. If you have fun with what you wear by mixing things up, you might find a new style that speaks to you!

HELP
PEOPLE

EVERY MORNING AT 5 A.M., Benjamin Franklin—an inventor, scientist, writer, and one of the Founding Fathers of the United States— woke up and asked himself, *"What good shall I do today?"* And each night, he asked himself, *"What good have I done today?"*

Doing good, being kind, and helping others, is a powerful way to make you feel better about the world and about yourself. If people around you are happy, you'll feel happy too! Research shows that spending money on others increases happiness more than spending it on yourself. Helping other people also allows you to feel closer and more connected with those around you. It gives us a feeling of purpose, making us feel more positive.

Empathy is understanding how other people are feeling. If you're feeling down, then other people might be feeling the same way, so why not see if you can make their day brighter?

Helping people ranges from hanging out the washing, to asking a friend if they're okay and really listening to their answer, spending time with your grandparents, or volunteering for a charity or organization. Here are some things you could do to make your family and the world happier.

HELP YOUR PARENTS

BEING USEFUL AND HELPFUL IS a wonderful feeling. We all have the power to do something for another person, no matter how small the act is. Why not start at home by helping your mom or dad?

SET THE TABLE FOR DINNER

Your parents probably often ask you to set the table before dinner. See if you can remember to do it without being asked. Make it a bit special by adding a vase of flowers to the table, candles, or folded napkins.

CLEAN UP AFTER DINNER

Your parents are probably pretty tired by the time they've worked all day and then gotten dinner on the table. After you've all finished eating, why not offer to clean up so they can sit down and relax?

MAKE BREAKFAST

Maybe on special occasions, like a birthday, Mother's Day, or Father's Day, your parents get treated to breakfast in bed. You could surprise them on another day by making them a special breakfast that shows how much you love them!

WASH THE CAR

Your parents would probably love a fresh, clean car, and washing the car is also a fun summer activity. With a bucket of soapy water, some wash cloths, and a good spray with the hose, you might even get clean too! While you're at it, you could give your bike or scooter a wash as well. If you're feeling up for it, you can also vacuum inside the car and clean the windows. Good job!

DO THE LAUNDRY

Have you ever used the washing machine? Perhaps you could find out how it works and help out with washing the clothes. There's something wonderful about the smell of freshly laundered clothing hanging in the sunshine to dry. Make sure to fold all the clothes neatly when they're dry.

PUT YOUR THINGS AWAY AND CLEAN YOUR ROOM

You've probably been asked to clean your room a million times before. See if you can do it without being asked, and maybe even jazz your room up a bit with some of the room-decorating ideas in this book!

WEED THE GARDEN

Along with getting you outdoors and being great exercise, helping out in the garden is something fun you can do that helps out your parents at the same time. It's lovely to be out in the sunshine, smell the freshly turned soil, and see your messy garden become neat. Use a small shovel to loosen the soil around the weeds, then use your fingers to pull the weeds out. Shake off the dirt around the roots, and place the weeds into a bucket to empty into your compost bin later. Once your garden is all weed-free, you could even freshen it up with some new seedlings or plants that you have rooted in water.

DOING SOMETHING NICE FOR SOMEONE ELSE

THERE'S NOTHING BETTER THAN WATCHING someone else feel happier because of something you have done. Think about some of the nice things you could do to help make another person's day brighter, whether that's helping a friend tidy their room, making a cake for someone, or offering to weed your elderly neighbor's garden. You have so much power to do good for others!

Here are some more nice things you could do for someone else:

- ✿ Make them a cup of tea
- ✿ Help put their groceries away
- ✿ Pick some flowers for their house
- ✿ Give up your seat on the bus
- ✿ Help with their homework
- ✿ Offer to share your snack with them
- ✿ Spend quality time with them

What are three things you love doing that you think could be of help to someone else?

DID YOU KNOW?

In 2020, during the coronavirus pandemic, people began putting teddy bears in their windows so when children who'd been stuck at home in lockdown went out for a walk, they could go on a bear hunt.

When William Winslow was just seven years old, he became determined to end childhood hunger in his North Carolina town. He partnered with a local grocery store to start a community food drive and collected 1,400 pounds of food. That first food drive became an annual event and now the teenager's organization **THE FOOD DRIVE KIDS** has collected more than $63,000 and 55,000 pounds of food to date. The Food Drive Kids continues to work on ending childhood hunger, rallying other young volunteers for the annual food drive, building school gardens, and setting up food pantries.

BE THE CHANGE COLORING CO. is a coloring book company that was started by four high school friends, Lauryn Hong, Ella Matlock, Sofia Migliazza, and Erin Rogers. They create fun coloring books that help educate children about modern issues while raising thousands of dollars to support various nonprofit organizations. What began as a school project has become a way to give back to their community.

Julia Warren is the founder of **CELEBRATE RVA**, a nonprofit organization she started as a sixteen-year-old after she met children who had never celebrated their birthdays. With the help of other volunteers, Celebrate RVA now gives more than 1,000 disadvantaged children in the Richmond, Virginia, area safe and fun birthday celebrations they may not have otherwise had. Julia believes everyone deserves to celebrate their birthday and that every child should experience joy on their special day.

INDEPENDENCE

IT'S NICE TO BE ABLE to care for other people, but always remember to care for yourself too. When you care for yourself and you're responsible for your own decisions, that's called independence. It takes practice to become independent, but most people find that as they learn to do things for themselves, they blossom and become more confident.

Start by taking small steps. If there's something your parents normally help you with, see if you can work out how to do it on your own—or ask someone to teach you how, so you can do it next time. This could be washing your own sheets one day, planning a meal you'd like to make, or helping shop for groceries. Other things you could learn to do around the house include changing a light bulb, fixing a leaky faucet, or painting the walls. You might like to take responsibility for a regular household chore, such as sweeping or mopping the floor, emptying the trash, or weeding the garden. If you have younger siblings, you could help feed, bathe, or entertain them. Even learning to entertain yourself is a type of independence, as is organizing your own homework and keeping track of your study time.

Independence is also about being able to take care of your health and your body. This can be as simple as brushing your teeth each day, washing your hair, remembering to stay hydrated, eating healthy food, exercising regularly, and getting the right amount of sleep.

When you manage these things for yourself, it means that you have the power to look after yourself, and that is a remarkable thing.

TIP

Ask for help when you need it!

It's wonderful to help others and be independent, but you'll need help sometimes too. Remember how good it feels to do something nice for someone else, and don't be afraid to ask someone to help you as well. We all need help sometimes.

HANNAH TAYLOR
Canada

On a freezing cold winter's night when she was five years old, Hannah saw a homeless man eating out of a dumpster. She was filled with sadness, and asked her mom why people couldn't just share what they had so no one had to live like this. Hannah's mom told her that maybe if Hannah could do something to help, then her heart wouldn't feel so sad. This moment started a passion in Hannah to help change the lives of homeless people. She asked her teacher if she could talk to her class about homelessness, and helped organize a fundraiser with her school. She then began to distribute jars to raise money among other schools and businesses. When she was eight, Hannah started The Ladybug Foundation, which spread awareness and raised money to help organizations that provide food and shelter to homeless people. The ladybug was their mascot because ladybugs bring good luck. They are also Hannah's favorite bug!

The Ladybug Foundation helped more than 65 different shelters, missions, food banks, and soup kitchens across Canada, and their motto was: "Share a little of what you have and care about each other always." When Hannah was ten years old, she was given a tour of a youth shelter in Toronto. She heard so many stories from young people about their favorite dinner they'd been given, but there was one girl who was very shy and quiet. Then, just as Hannah was about to leave, the girl gave her a hug and said, "Before today I thought nobody loved me, and now I know you do."

Hannah is now twenty-four years old and studying law. She hopes to use her career to continue to help Canadians who are homeless or living in poverty. As she says, "Your voice is powerful right now. You don't have to wait until you're older."

FIGHTING FOR A CAUSE YOU CARE ABOUT

IT'S A WONDERFUL FEELING TO be able to do good in the world and work with others toward a goal that you all believe in. When we follow our passions, we feel lighter and more motivated—we get that feeling that we want to leap out of bed the minute we wake up! Sometimes, our passions can be fighting for causes through volunteering or raising money.

Here are some examples of how you might tackle certain issues and give back to your community.

- ❀ Raise awareness at your school about the problems caused by single-use plastics, and how to avoid them, for example by having discussions with your friends, putting up posters, and making speeches.
- ❀ Donate unwanted toys and clothes to charity.
- ❀ Bake cookies or muffins to give to volunteers, such as firefighters and emergency service workers.
- ❀ Volunteer at your local animal shelter.
- ❀ Organize a beach, river, or park clean up day with your friends.
- ❀ Raise money for a charity of your choice by participating in a fun-run or having a bake sale.
- ❀ When it's your birthday, ask your friends and family to donate to a charity you care about or sponsor an animal or a child in need instead of giving you a gift.
- ❀ Volunteer to plant trees.

Alysa Monteagudo launched the student-led organization **SO SHE CAN** with co-founder Celine. so she CAN aims to amplify the stories of underrepresented voices and empower marginalized communities by raising awareness and cultivating a community of positivity through their blog articles, social media posts, and podcasts.

Jaylen Arnold, the creator of **JAYLEN'S CHALLENGE FOUNDATION**, started speaking out against bullying when he was only eight years old. Jaylen was bullied by classmates because he was different—he was diagnosed with Tourette Syndrome, Asperger's Syndrome, and Obsessive-Compulsive Disorder when he was very young. Jaylen has made it his mission to make sure no other child goes through a similar experience, promoting awareness and rallying students to prevent bullying of differently abled kids around the world.

Joshua Williams founded the nonprofit organization **JOSHUA'S HEART FOUNDATION** in Miami, Florida, in 2005. JHF is a youth-run organization that helps stomp out hunger in underprivileged communities around the world by providing necessities like groceries and other types of aid. Thousands of volunteers lead fundraisers, distribute food, and educate their peers about global hunger. JHF has inspired young people to become changemakers and start their own chapters of Joshua's Heart in their communities.

Prajnal Jain, a formerly undocumented South Asian immigrant, began an anti-cyberbullying campaign when she was twelve years old and continues to advocate for womxn's empowerment, founding **GLOBAL GIRLHOOD**. Global Girlhood's mission is to inspire storytelling and create a global online community using social media as a tool for positive change, encouraging intercultural dialogue and connecting people of every background and ethnicity— despite geographical location.

HELP THE PLANET

YOU MIGHT NOT KNOW IT, but living a more mindful life is one simple step we can all take toward helping the planet. When we slow down and focus on the little things in life that make us happy, we become more aware of the Earth and the impact we're having on it. Watching the clouds, stargazing, birdwatching, hiking, listening to the waves at the beach—all of these things connect us to nature and make us want to protect it.

Helping the planet makes us feel more connected to the environment, and living a more sustainable life gives us a sense of purpose and helps us be more optimistic about the future. We're all living on the Earth together and so we should take care of it together. This makes us focus on something bigger than ourselves, which in turn makes our worries and problems seem a littler smaller. Here are some mindfulness activities you can do that help the planet, so you can be part of the mission to keep Earth safe.

LACHLAN WATSON
Australia

At a charity repair workshop in Sydney, Australia, Lachlan Watson
can be found fixing items that would otherwise be thrown away.
The Bower Reuse and Repair Centre is an award-winning environmental
charity that's committed to reducing landfill. On top of that, they promote
creativity and initiative, encouraging people to upcycle the things they own
rather than putting broken items in the trash. Once a week after school,
Lachy volunteers there where he specializes in fixing iPhones and computers
and helps combat throw-away culture.

**1. How old are you now and how old were you when you started
working at the Bower Reuse and Repair Centre?**

I'm thirteen years old now. I was about ten when I started at The Bower.

2. Where did you grow up and how did that inspire you?

I grew up in Sydney's Inner West neighborhood, in Annandale. Twelve
months ago, we moved to Lilyfield. My inspiration started when I was seven,
when my dad's iPhone 3GS broke and we decided to take it apart and fix it.

**3. What made you want to work at The Bower, and what's your favorite
thing about working there now?**

I'd already been fixing devices for about a year and a half, and one of
my godparents, Christine, introduced me to The Bower. I loved the idea
that I could get devices (or basically any second-hand stuff, but it was
the computers, monitors, consoles, etc. that interested me) for cheaper
than what most people sell them for on eBay. I was nine the first time I
went to The Bower and asked for a job, and I was told maybe when I was

a bit older. About three months later, Griffin, the electrical manager, let me join but then canceled as they weren't ready and were moving locations. About a year later, we got a call from Griffin saying that I could come and volunteer at their new repair cafe. My favorite thing about working at The Bower is doing what I love—tinkering and repairing, solving problems, and making things usable for people again.

4. **Why do you like repairing things? Why is it important to reuse and repair?**
I find it interesting to see how things do or don't work. Even big brands sometimes come up with poor designs. People soon want to get rid of them, so many end up at The Bower.

It's important to reuse and repair as 50 million tons of eWaste (electronic waste) is created every year and 20 percent of it is not properly recycled. A large amount of this could be easily fixed.

5. **What's your favorite pastime or hobby?**
In my spare time, I like cycling, hanging out with friends, and repairing electronics.

6. **How do you stay positive when times are tough?**
I talk to friends or my parents about how I'm feeling and ask for advice.

7. **What would you say is your biggest achievement so far?**
I'd probably say that my biggest achievement is rescuing a bunch of functional iMacs from my old school and being able to donate them to people in need.

8. **Do you have any tips to help kids live on the bright side?**
If you're feeling down or upset, try to do things that you love or find relaxing.

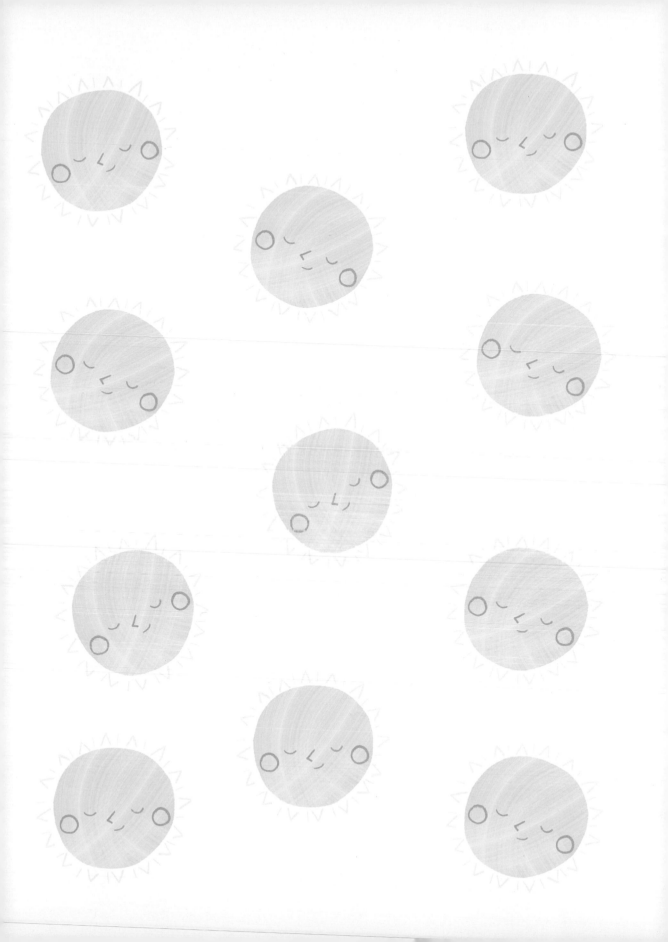

GOING
ON A
GARBAGE
WALK

NEXT TIME YOU'RE GOING OUT with your friends, why not turn the excursion into a garbage walk? It's okay: the walk won't actually be garbage, you'll just be picking some of it up to make your neighborhood and the world a cleaner place.

Walking is great exercise, and if you pick up trash along the way it's great for the environment too. It's also a good way to get friends together around a shared goal, and even make new friends.

For your garbage walk, you'll need:

- ❀ Comfy clothing and footwear
- ❀ Sun protection
- ❀ A pair of gloves
- ❀ A bag or bucket to put any trash you collect in

You can go around your neighborhood, to a nearby park, beach, nature preserve or playground, or walk around your school. Ask your friends and family and other kids at your school to get involved too—why not start a garbage club!

GOING ON A BIKE RIDE

INSTEAD OF DRIVING SOMEWHERE TO hang out, see if there's a place you want to go that's close by, so you can ride your bike there instead.

SHARING IS CARING

DO YOU HAVE TOYS YOU no longer want, clothes you've outgrown (or just don't like!), or books you've already read? Instead of throwing them away, give them to a charity or organize a swap with friends and friends of friends. Buying brand new things all the time is wasteful, especially when we all own so much stuff already!

YOU HAVE SO MUCH POWER when it comes to helping your parents care for the planet! When you go to the grocery store, make sure you get your parents to take their reusable bags. Remind them to avoid using plastic produce bags and discourage them from buying packaged fruit and vegetables.

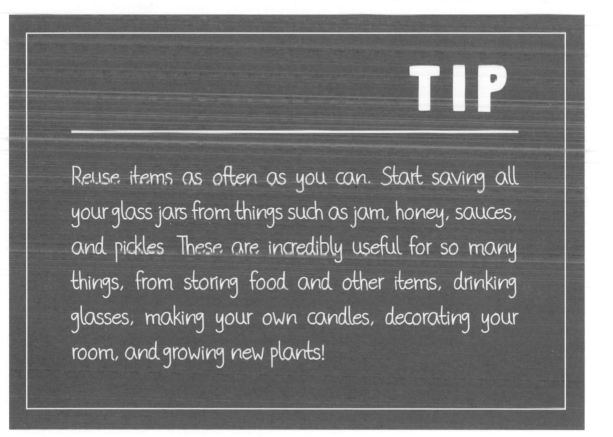

TIP

Reuse items as often as you can. Start saving all your glass jars from things such as jam, honey, sauces, and pickles These are incredibly useful for so many things, from storing food and other items, drinking glasses, making your own candles, decorating your room, and growing new plants!

PLANT
A TREE

TREES ARE VITAL FOR THE EARTH. Without them, life couldn't continue. They're the biggest plants on the planet, and have been called the lungs of the Earth because through their leaves they produce oxygen and trap (or "sequester") harmful particles out of the air we breathe.

When they grow, trees absorb carbon dioxide that they store in their wood. Excess carbon dioxide is building up in our atmosphere and contributing to climate change. To help slow the rate of global warming, the more trees we have the better. Trees can even reduce the temperature in cities because they release water vapor into the air and their leaves reflect heat upward!

As well as helping the climate, trees give native animals a place to live. After wildfires, when their woodland homes have been destroyed, creatures need trees more than ever. every tree counts. Across the planet, trees provide fruit as well as nuts, spices, maple syrup, and the all important chocolate, and their roots hold soil in place, reducing flooding and erosion.

Trees and green spaces have a relaxing effect on people, lowering our stress levels and increasing our feelings of wellbeing. Is there anything trees can't do?

Now that we know how important trees are, we need to work together to protect them for our future. Around the world, many different communities and organizations are dedicated to planting more trees. People of all cultures, ages, and genders come together around tree-planting, empowered by the way trees help improve our quality of life. You can get involved too, for example by making a donation to a tree-planting organization, or helping raise awareness among others about the importance of trees.

By helping to grow trees, you're making a positive difference in the world. In turn, that makes a positive difference in your life.

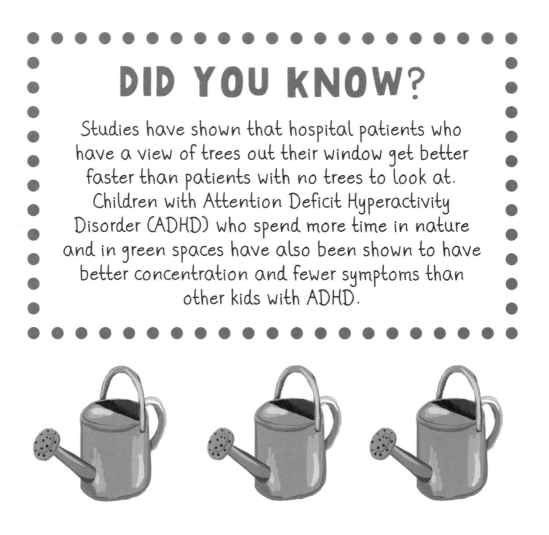

DID YOU KNOW?

Studies have shown that hospital patients who have a view of trees out their window get better faster than patients with no trees to look at. Children with Attention Deficit Hyperactivity Disorder (ADHD) who spend more time in nature and in green spaces have also been shown to have better concentration and fewer symptoms than other kids with ADHD.

ACTIVITY: PLANT A TREE

Plant a special tree that's all yours. Take a photo of your sapling once a week to keep track of its progress.

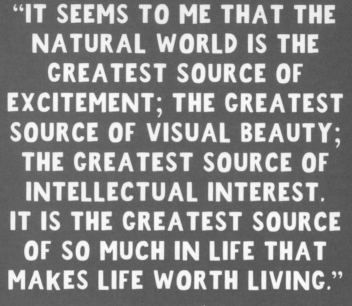

"IT SEEMS TO ME THAT THE NATURAL WORLD IS THE GREATEST SOURCE OF EXCITEMENT; THE GREATEST SOURCE OF VISUAL BEAUTY; THE GREATEST SOURCE OF INTELLECTUAL INTEREST. IT IS THE GREATEST SOURCE OF SO MUCH IN LIFE THAT MAKES LIFE WORTH LIVING."

—DAVID ATTENBOROUGH, ENGLISH BROADCASTER, WRITER, AND NATURAL HISTORIAN

DANTE VERGARA
Chile

Dante is an eleven-year-old environmental activist from Chile.
He's known as Chile's youngest "bug-ologist" (bichólogo in Spanish),
a word he made up to describe his passion for bugs. He first became
interested in tiny creatures when he found a tarantula in his
grandmother's garden! Because of his love of entomology (the study of
insects), Dante became interested in climate change.

Always an avid explorer, at four years old Dante started a blog to teach
other kids about insects and animals. He began featuring videos of his
adventures into the hills around Santiago, where he captures insects,
small reptiles, and amphibians, studies and talks about them, then
releases them. In his videos, Dante fearlessly holds snakes,
spots birds, and explains to his audience what he knows about each
creature's habitat and what they eat. Dante believes that to protect
nature, we must know it.

In November 2019, Dante was named as an ambassador of COP25
(the 2019 United Nations Climate Change Conference). He spoke before
the UN General Assembly to call on countries to formally recognize our
right to a healthy environment: clean air and water, healthy food, a
stable climate, and healthy biodiversity and ecosystems. When fifteen-
year-old actor and UNICEF Goodwill Ambassador Millie Bobby Brown
introduced Dante onto the stage, she said that "no one knows better
than him that small things can have a big impact."

ISRA HIRSI
United States of America

Environmental and racial justice have always been important to Isra Hirsi. Growing up in Minnesota as a black Muslim girl and daughter of U.S. Congresswoman Ilhan Omar, Isra has been conscious of racial justice issues not only in her community but around the country and the world since she was very young. She says she grew up in a family where being a changemaker was the norm and she organized her first rally in the ninth grade. Her experiences feeling that she often was the only young BIPOC (Black, Indigenous, or Person of Color) in the environmental movement inspired her to cofound the U.S. Youth Climate Strike organization in 2019 when she was only 16. The U.S. Youth Climate Strike organized student protests and walks calling for climate action, in nearly every state in the U.S., and in over 47 countries worldwide.

So far in her journey of achieving environmental and racial justice, Isra has collaborated with indigenous people and stood with them in their protests against the Minnesota oil pipelines, participated in Black Lives Matter protests, shared a TED talk about The Angry Black Girl, and has spoken at numerous national and international conferences about climate change and racial justice.

Isra continues her important work today, explaining at the 2021 #RaceAnd: Our Present, Our Future conference: "Our future depends on the conversations and actions we take right now at our present moment in history. Young activists leading the way with learnings from those who have walked this path will ensure we achieve a world where all people can thrive."

A PLASTIC-FREE PICNIC

WE ALL KNOW THAT WE need to work on cutting back how much plastic we use—from shopping bags and produce bags to straws, cups, plates and cutlery, water bottles; the list goes on! Almost all of this plastic eventually ends up in landfills or in the ocean, where it's incredibly harmful to the marine creatures and sea birds.

Think of some activities in your life when normally lots of plastic would be used and try incorporating some plastic-free options. Here's everything you need to go on a plastic-free picnic!

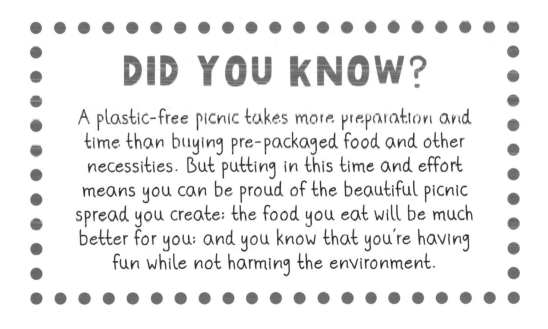

DID YOU KNOW?

A plastic-free picnic takes more preparation and time than buying pre-packaged food and other necessities. But putting in this time and effort means you can be proud of the beautiful picnic spread you create; the food you eat will be much better for you; and you know that you're having fun while not harming the environment.

FIRST STEPS

❀ Invite family or friends who are excited to do this with you! This will bring you all together around a shared goal.

❀ Pick a time, date, and place that works for everyone.

❀ Plan ahead—decide what each person is going to make, and who's bringing what.

❀ Once you know what you're making, plan a trip to a grocery store with a bulk food section to buy your ingredients. If you're buying things like flour and sugar, take clean containers that can be weighed by the cashier before you begin shopping. Then fill them with as much as you need, and the weight of the container is subtracted so you only pay for the ingredient.

THINGS TO AVOID (AND BETTER ALTERNATIVES)

❀ **Ziploc bags and plastic wrap:** Instead, put your sandwiches in a paper bag, lunchbox, or wrap them in cloth (which can then double as a napkin!).

❀ **Plastic cutlery and plates:** Bring cutlery and plates from home, or look into buying biodegradable paper or bamboo alternatives.

❀ **Single-use plastic cups and straws:** Get everyone to bring their own reusable water bottle, or you can repurpose jam and honey jars as glasses. If you really want to use straws, choose reusable stainless-steel ones, or see if you can buy biodegradable ones.

❀ **Bread bags:** Buy your bread from a bakery and ask them to pack it in a paper bag for you. Or look into making your own bread!

PREPARING YOUR FOOD ————————————

Use the recipes on the following pages, or come up with some of your own!

EGG SALAD SANDWICHES

Simple and delicious!

What you'll need:

- 8 free-range or pastured eggs
- 2–3 tablespoons mayonnaise (buy it in a glass jar that you can reuse, or look into making your own!)
- 1 teaspoon Dijon mustard
- salt and pepper to season
- 1 tablespoon finely chopped chives (optional)
- 8 slices fresh bread
- lettuce, tomato, and cucumber to serve (optional)

Makes: 4 sandwiches

What to do:

1. To hard-boil the eggs, place them in a saucepan and fill the saucepan with water until it's covering the eggs by a couple of inches.

2. Over high heat, bring the water to a rolling boil. Put the lid on the saucepan, cook for another 30 seconds, then move the pan off the heat. Set a timer for 10–12 minutes, depending on if you're using small or large eggs.

3. Remove the eggs with a slotted spoon and place them in iced water to cool.

4. Once the eggs are cooled, peel them and place them in a bowl.

5. With a fork, gently mash up the eggs until they're still a little chunky. Add in your mayonnaise, Dijon, salt and pepper, and chives, if using, and mix to combine.

6. Spread your egg mixture onto 4 of the bread slices to make 4 sandwiches. Add lettuce, tomato, or cucumber, if using.

SAVORY MUFFINS

These delicious muffins taste best still warm from the oven, but they're tasty when eaten cold too!

What you'll need:

- 2 eggs
- ⅓ cup milk
- ¼ cup butter, melted
- 2 spring onions, chopped
- 1 cup baby spinach, chopped
- ½ red bell pepper, finely chopped
- 2 strips bacon, finely diced (tip: take your own container to the deli at your local supermarket, and ask if they'll use that instead of wrapping the bacon in a plastic bag)
- ½ cup grated cheese
- 1 cup self-rising flour
- salt and pepper to season

Makes: 12

What to do:

1. Pre-heat the oven to 350°F. Line a 12-cup muffin pan and lightly grease the liners.

2. In a large bowl, lightly whisk the eggs then mix in the milk and melted butter.

3. Add the spring onion, spinach, pepper, bacon, and cheese, and stir through.

4. Add in the flour, salt, and pepper to taste, then mix until the ingredients are just combined.

5. Divide the mixture evenly between the muffin cups—about 1 tbsp per cup—and bake in the oven for 20 minutes, or until a skewer stuck in the middle comes out clean.

6. Allow to cool in the pan for 10 minutes. Then remove, and enjoy!

STICKS AND DIPS

Get crunching on these veggie sticks, perfect for digging into this smooth avo dip. If you're feeling adventurous, try making your own sweet potato wedges too!

Serves: 4

What you'll need:

- 1 large carrot
- 2 or 3 celery sticks
- 2 avocados
- 3 tablespoons sour cream
- 2 tablespoons lime juice
- 2 tablespoons chopped cilantro (optional)
- salt and pepper to season

What to do:

1. Chop up your carrot and celery into small sticks.

2. Cut the avocados in half, remove the pit, then scoop the soft part out of the skin and into a bowl.

3. Using a fork, mix in the sour cream, lime juice, and cilantro (if using), and season with salt and pepper to taste. Mix until the dip is smooth.

PEANUT BUTTER COOKIES

Makes: 24

You won't be able to get enough of these cookies!

What you'll need:

- ⅔ cup unsalted butter, slightly softened
- ½ cup crunchy peanut butter
- ¾ cup brown sugar
- ¾ cup white sugar
- 2 eggs
- 1½ cups plain flour
- 1 teaspoon baking powder
- 1½ teaspoons baking soda
- a pinch of salt

What to do:

1. In the bowl of an electric mixer, combine the butter, peanut butter, brown sugar, and white sugar, and mix until light and creamy.

2. Beat in the eggs one at a time.

3. In a separate bowl, sift the flour, baking powder, baking soda, and salt, and mix together. Stir this into the butter mixture to form a dough. Cover dough and put in the fridge for about 1 hour.

4. Preheat the oven to 350°F, and line a baking tray with parchment paper.

5. Roll the dough into balls that are about an inch in diameter. Place them on the tray, leaving a couple of inches between each dough ball. Using a fork, press down on the top of each dough ball to flatten it.

6. Bake for about 15–20 minutes or until the cookies are just beginning to brown. Remove from the oven and allow the cookies to cool for 10 minutes before removing them from the tray.

HOMEMADE SUMMER LEMONADE

For a special treat, it's nice to have a fancy drink—such as orange juice or one of the juice recipes on page 162. This thirst-quenching homemade summer lemonade is perfect for a picnic. If you have access to a lemon tree and can use fresh lemons, even better! Bring it along in a reusable bottle or repurposed jar.

What you'll need:

- 1 cup granulated sugar
- 1 cup water
- 1 cup freshly squeezed lemon juice (the juice of about 4–6 lemons)
- 2 cups cold water
- plenty of ice for serving

Makes: 4 cups

What to do:

1. Place the sugar and water in a small saucepan over low heat and bring to a simmer, stirring until the sugar is completely dissolved. Be careful as the syrup will be very hot.

2. Into a large jug, pour the lemon juice and sugar syrup, then add 2 cups of cold water and mix well to combine.

3. Pour into four small jars to take on your picnic, or if drinking right away, add ice to your glasses. If you prefer your lemonade less lemony, just add a bit more cold water or ice.

LEMONADE

PLASTIC-FREE PICNIC TIPS

- ✿ Any unpackaged fruit is the perfect plastic-free snack!
- ✿ If there's a bulk food store near you, ask your parents to take you there to buy things like nuts and dried fruit. Unpackaged chocolate might be available too!
- ✿ Bring food and drinks in repurposed glass jars.
- ✿ Make sure you bring a few containers to take home any leftovers so you don't contribute to food waste.
- ✿ Remember to pack a picnic blanket with enough space for everyone, some outdoor games, and plenty of sun protection!

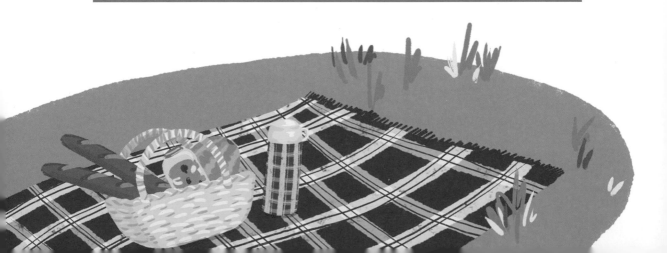

TIP

We have a lot of power when we shop. Every time someone offers you a plastic bag and you say no, it's a win for the environment. As more and more of us say no to single-use plastic items, together we can help stop them from ending up in our water, where they harm sea creatures.

THE POWER IS IN YOUR HANDS

There are countless easy and fun ways that you can help the environment. This could be always turning off the lights when you leave a room, taking shorter showers, setting up a worm farm or composting system to reduce your food waste, and buying less. It's up to you to go forth and do the things you can do to help make our planet a better place.

RESOURCES

BRIGHT SPARKS

Aelita Andre
aelitaandre.com
instagram.com/aelitaandre
facebook.com/aelitaandreartist

Alysa Monteagudo and Celine
soshecan.wixsite.com

Coco Gauff
instagram.com/cocogauff

Dante Vergara
bichologia.com
youtube.com/Bicholog%C3%ADa

Haile Thomas
hailevthomas.com
instagram.com/hailethomas

Henry Patterson
notbeforetea.co.uk
instagram.com/not_before_tea

Isra Hirsi
instagram.com/israhirsi

Jaylen Arnold
jaylenschallenge.org

Joshua Williams
joshuasheart.org

Julia Warren
celebraterva.org

Kate Barry
scrunchiemunchies.com.au
instagram.com/scrunchiemunchieaus
facebook.com/scrunchiemunchies

Lauryn Hong, Ella Matlock, Sofia Migliazza, and Erin Rogers
bethechangecoloringco.com

Mo Bridges
mosbowsmemphis.com
instagram.com/mosbowsmemphis

Prajnal Jain
globalgirlhood.org

William Winslow
thefooddrivekids.org

ORGANIZATIONS

Mindful Schools
mindfulschools.org

IWRITE
iwrite.org

Harmony Project
harmonyproject.org

WHERE TO GO FOR HELP

The Jed Foundation
jedfoundation.org

NIDA for Teens
teens.drugabuse.gov

The Trevor Project
trevorproject.org

USEFUL APPS AND WEBSITES ———————————

Meditation:
Smiling Mind
Headspace

Stargazing:
SkyView Lite
Star Walk 2

Language:
Duolingo

Music:
Spotify

Coding:
Scratch
Code.org

TED-Ed:
Ed.ted.com

ACKNOWLEDGMENTS

No amount of thanks seems enough to convey the gratitude I have for my team at Pantera Press. The Greens: Ali, Marty, John, and Jenny, your support is more appreciated than I can express in words, and I'm so glad to have found my way into the Pantera family. Lex Hirst, your passion is inspiring, and I'm very lucky to have you as my publisher. To my editor, Anne Reilly, your careful guidance, and boundless enthusiasm and excitement for this book, made it such a joy to work with you.

My thanks to Anna Blackie—your encouragement, friendship, and ability to make me laugh uncontrollably even in the most stressful times mean so much to me. To Katy McEwen, rights manager extraordinaire! I never dreamed that my book would end up being sold around the world, but you made that happen, and I'm so grateful. And to the rest of my team for working to see my book onto shelves and into the hands of readers—Lucy Barrett, Kajal Narayan, Léa Antigny, and Kirsty van der Veer—my heartfelt thanks.

This book would be nowhere near as beautiful without my cover designer and illustrator Astred Hicks, and my internals designer, Elysia Clapin. Thanks to both of you, my book looks like a beacon of joy!

To my proofreader, Vanessa Lanaway, for your keen eyes and positive words. Thanks to Jayneen Sanders, for being the inspiration behind the pirate stance in the yoga section.

To these incredible young people, who were sparks of positivity while I was writing: Aelita Andre, Kate Barry, Lachlan Watson, Haile Thomas, Coco Gauff, Simba, Isra Hirsi, Lorena Ramírez, William Winslow, Lauryn Hong, Ella Matlock, Sofia Migliazza, Erin Rogers, Julia Warren, Alysa Monteagudo and Celine,

Jaylen Arnold, Joshua Williams, Prajnal Jain, Henry Patterson, Akim Camara, Mo Bridges, Dante Vergara, and Hannah Taylor. My thanks also to Mindful Schools, iWRITE, and Harmony Project—these wonderful organizations make the world a happier place for kids.

To you, my reader, a big thank you for picking up this book. I hope that it's helped you find a little more happiness in the world.

My parents, Francesca and Adrian. There is so much of my childhood in this book, and that is thanks to you, for giving me the freedom to lie in the sun on the verandah and dream about life rather than spend too much time in it. And to Chip, Maddy, Jerry, and Olivia for lying in the sun with me.

And last, but not least, James Searle, my favorite picnic companion. I dedicated this book to you because my world is brighter with you in it. The comfort of making our life together and the joy we find in the small moments, like cooking, cleaning, and growing plants, mean everything to me. Whatever the future holds, I know everything will be okay with you by my side.

ABOUT THE AUTHOR

Lucy Bell is an author, book editor, and music teacher on a journey to live a more ethical, sustainable, and mindful life.

After getting her Bachelor of Arts degree at the University of Sydney with majors in English and Ancient History, Lucy earned a Master of Publishing. Now she works for a social-purpose publishing house making big differences and helping fund not-for-profits and charities to close the literacy gap.

Lucy grew up on the New South Wales Central Coast in Australia surrounded by four siblings, a cat, two dogs, two sheep, a lizard, lots of guinea pigs, and thirteen chickens. She now lives in Sydney and while watering her balcony garden, dreams of one day owning her own country farmhouse.

Lucy is also the author of *You Can Change the World*, which was the winner of the 2020 Nautilus Book Awards as well as the 2021 Green Earth Book Award. *You Can Change the World* was also shortlisted for the ABIA Small Publishers' Children's Book of the Year 2020, the Australian Book Design Award for Best Designed Children's Non-Fiction Illustrated Book 2020, and the Wilderness Society's Environment Award for Children's Literature 2020.

AUTHOR'S NOTE

As you go through life, always remember to take a deep breath when everything feels too big and worrisome. Think about the good things in your life that make you happy, and make time for the people you love, the activities you love doing, and for following your passions.

Maybe the thing you love doing hasn't even been mentioned in this book, and you're still looking for it. Whatever it is, when you find it, make sure you hold on to it. Then you'll always have a way to live on the bright side when you need it.